Global Content Marketing

How to Create Great Content, Reach More Customers, and Build a Worldwide Marketing Strategy That Works

Pam Didner

Mc
Graw
Hill
Education

New York   Chicago   San Francisco   Athens   London   Madrid
Mexico City   Milan   New Delhi   Singapore   Sydney   Toronto

1 2 3 4 5 6 7 8 9 0   DOC/DOC   1 2 0 9 8 7 6 5 4

ISBN: 978-0-07-184097-2
MHID: 0-07-184097-4

e-ISBN: 978-0-07-184098-9
e-MHID: 0-07-184098-2

McGraw-Hill Education books are available at special quantity discounts to use as premiums and sales promotions, or for use in corporate training programs. To contact a representative please e-mail us at bulksales@mcgraw-hill.com.

謹於此書獻給我的父母：謝福助老師和邱鍛美女士

For Mom and Dad: Du-Mei and Fu-Chu Hsieh

And for my husband, Michael

CONTENTS

PREFACE

The Internet is our oyster. We can find almost anything as long as we are connected to the web. There is no shortage of content and information around the world.

As of January 11, 2014, there were 1.61 billion indexed web pages according to www.worldwidewebsize.com, which provides the daily estimated number of pages on the Internet.

The truth is, while the Internet is our oyster, the pearl is now the mobile device. According to the U.N. telecom agency, "there were about 7 billion [cell phone] subscriptions in 2013"—roughly 96 out of 100 people on this planet have at least one cell phone.[1][2] With the Internet and a smartphone, not only can we access almost any information, we can also connect with anyone, anywhere on this planet, as long as he or she has a device to access the Internet. I am always in awe of how a simple touch or swipe on a handheld device serves as an instant gateway to human knowledge and interaction.

> *The truth is, while the Internet is our oyster, the pearl is now the mobile device.*

Who Should Read This Book

In the borderless virtual world, your customers can come from unexpected places. This book shares the process of using content as a marketing mechanism to grow your business by expanding to audiences outside of your countries, regardless of the size of

[1] ITU World Telecommunication/ICT Indicators database, http://www.itu.int/en/ITU-D/Statistics/Pages/stat/default.aspx, December 2013
[2] Shea Bennett, *Social Media – a History*, http://www.mediabistro.com/alltwitter/social-media-1969-2012_b45869, Mediabistro, July 4, 2013

your company. This book is targeted towards practitioners and presents a planning and synthesis process to help you scale content and marketing across regions. This includes recent college graduates who want to pursue a career in marketing, entrepreneurs trying to maximize the chances for a successful venture, and agency marketers that consult, strategize, and implement cross-regional content marketing for their clients.

What This Book Is

This book assumes you've already had an introduction to basic marketing concepts and will give you strategies and knowledge needed to scale your content globally. After finishing this book, you will:

- ▶ Become a better synthesizer with the ability to make your content marketing effective across regions.
- ▶ Evaluate and question your marketing strategies from a content marketing perspective.
- ▶ Be able to identify key actions and strategies to apply to your projects or your roles.
- ▶ Be a better marketer by identifying the dots you have never connected before.

What This Book Is Not

When you read through the book, you will notice each company's or individual's content strategies and executions are different and situational. You need to extrapolate the ideas and processes so they apply to your companies, your clients, or your roles.

Content marketing is a broad field, and I can't cover everything in one book. Below is a list of topics that are touched upon in this book, but they are not focus areas:

- ▶ Brand, visual and writing style guide creation
- ▶ Search engine optimization (SEO) and search engine marketing (SEM)

- ▶ Software recommendations for content planning, production, and measurement
- ▶ Software recommendations for content localization and translation
- ▶ Web and mobile app design
- ▶ User experience design
- ▶ Social media marketing
- ▶ In-depth marketing analytics

The 4 P's for Global Content Marketing

We have heard of the 4 P's of the marketing mix, which are Product, Promote, Place, and Price. These 4 P's have been the cornerstone of modern marketing. Inspired by the 4 P's, I created a new set of 4 P's for global content marketing: Plan, Produce (used here as a verb and pronounced pruh-**doos**), Promote, and Perfect (used here as a verb and pronounced per-**fekt**). This book uses these 4 P's as a guide to the global content marketing cycle from planning your content strategy to measuring the impact of content.

- ▶ Plan: Set up strategy before execution
- ▶ Produce: Create content that matters
- ▶ Promote: Distribute content in the digital era
- ▶ Perfect: Measure and optimize to drive maximum impact

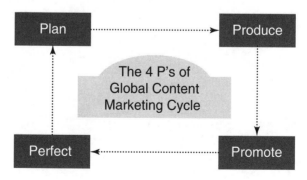

FIGURE 0.01 Pam Didner's 4 P's of the Global Content Marketing Cycle

But Wait, There's More

Two additional chapters are included to address the skill sets of future content marketers and my thoughts on the future of content marketing. I also created a companion Web site to this book: http://www.globalcontent.marketing, which provides supplemental materials that you are welcome to use in presentations or as part of a business case as long as you credit the source.

And Now,

Dive in and enjoy! Feel free to tweet, or post your thoughts about this book on LinkedIn, Facebook, Tumblr, your blog, or other social media platforms. You can always reach me through www.pamdidner.com. Love to hear from you.

@PamDidner #contentMKT or #globalMKT

The Internet Has No Borders

"No man is an island, entire of itself;
Every man is a piece of the continent,
a part of the main..."

—JOHN DONNE

The geographical boundaries that separate us physically do not really exist on the Internet. Like it or not, we are connected virtually, once we are online. Of course, this is not why John Donne wrote his verses in 1623,[1] yet his words coincidently and accurately describe the current phenomena: "No man is an island entire of itself; every man is a piece of the continent, a part of the main. . . ." *Every time I read his words, I can't help but change "a part of the main" to "a part of the Net."*

The Internet has no borders or boundaries. OK, I take that back. Some countries try to impose borders and boundaries online. But as long as a company has an online presence, and as long as its products can be shipped and services performed remotely or virtually, a core audience can be reached anywhere.

---

[1]John Donne, Meditation XVII, http://en.wikipedia.org/wiki/Meditation_XVII, Wikipedia

Here is a great example: Joe Nevin's Bumps for Boomers ski program in Aspen, Colorado. Joe noticed a lack of ski programs targeting baby boomers. As an avid skier and a baby boomer himself, he noticed competent baby boomer skiers (born between 1946–1964) were averse to expert-level skiing. Due to a fear of getting injured and lack of confidence and skills, baby boomers tended to avoid mogul skiing and powder. Joe developed a four-day ski program with instruction and structured practices to teach intermediate baby boomer skiers how to safely navigate moguls and powder. He applied his expertise to create more than 300 useful and educational content pieces[2] in various formats and topics to help baby boomers improve their skills. Those finding the content compelling can easily sign up for a course.

Joe's program launched in 2002. The business has been growing 12 percent year after year. To his surprise, customers come from all over the world, from as far away as the United Kingdom, Australia, and Russia. Keep in mind, Joe Nevin's Bumps for Boomers, LLC is a typical small business, not a big enterprise.

So what's his secret weapon? While Joe's Web site is only in English, he reaches customers worldwide via the numerous pieces of content he uploads to his Web site, biweekly e-mails, and SEO. Although the Web site which is English only is not ideal, there are tools available, like Google Translate, which makes it accessible to a foreign audience. In addition, some videos are done in a show-and-tell style, which minimizes language barriers. By sharing useful and educational content, Joe has positioned Bumps for Boomers as *the* resource for skiing programs and information for a very specific target audience. This is a perfect example of a small business breaking through physical and national boundaries through content marketing, even though it's only in one language.

---

[2] direct interview with Joe Nevin

Three Key Terms: Content, Content Marketing, and Global Content Marketing

Content can be a video, a blog, a post, an image, a webinar, a tweet, a white paper, an e-book, a coupon, or even a piece of music. Newspapers, books, flyers, and pamphlets are also forms of content. Thus, **content is everywhere**. Here is a succinct definition of content by Erin Kissane, author of *The Elements of Content Strategy*: "In the web industry, anything that conveys meaningful information to humans is called content."[3]

> *Content can be a video, a blog, a post, an image, a webinar, a tweet, a white paper, an e-book, a coupon, or even a piece of music.*

Some authors define content strategy and planning specifically for web design and user interface. Having a solid content plan as part of web design and user interface is indeed vital. In this book, however, I look at content strategy through different lenses. To create a global content plan, we need to move the content discussion **upstream** as part of a bigger marketing plan process. I will explain this in Chapter 4.

For **content marketing**, I find Amanda Maksymiw's definition hits the core: "the process of developing and sharing relevant, valuable, and engaging content to target audience with the goal of acquiring new customers or increasing business from existing customers."[4]

My definition of **global content marketing** simply builds upon Maksymiw's: "Global content marketing is the process of developing and sharing relevant, valuable, and engaging content with target audiences **across countries** with the goal of acquiring new customers or increasing business from existing customers **globally**."

With companies moving into new territories in order to grow, it's important to assess the existing content inventory, future content marketing strategy, and plan to better support the marketing needs of new regions. After all, many businesses

[3] Erin Kissane, *The Elements of Content Strategy*, p. 1, 2011
[4] Joe Pulizzi, six useful content marketing definitions, http://contentmarketinginstitute.com/2012/06/content-marketing-definition/

have limited budgets and resources. We need to assess the inventory to determine what content pieces can be reused and repackaged and what content pieces need to be customized or created for local usage. Not every content piece can be scaled across regions. Collaboration and conversation between the headquarters and local teams are essential. The ultimate goal is to create the right content in the right channel so your audience can find it at the right time. This is a lofty goal. It's easy to say and hard to implement, especially in a global context.

Global Content Marketing Is About Connecting the Dots

"Creativity is just connecting things. When you ask creative people how they did something, they feel a little guilty because they didn't really do it, they just saw something. It seemed obvious to them after a while. That's because they were able to connect experiences they've had and synthesize new things." Steve Jobs' quote reminds me of a quote from the Bible, Ecclesiastes 1:9: "What has been will be again, what has been done will be done again; there is nothing new under the sun." Innovation and inspiration comes from connecting dots that seem unrelated. A telephone and a copy machine evolved into a fax machine. A phone, a camera, and an online banking app enable online deposits. A phone displaying a quick response (QR) code becomes an airline boarding pass.

> *Innovation and inspiration comes from connecting dots that seem unrelated. A telephone and a copy machine evolved into a fax machine.*

"Connecting the dots" also applies on the global content marketing front. Five blog posts from the United States and third-party research reports from China and Germany can become one short e-book in three languages. One 10-page white paper with case studies from three countries can easily become three infographics, one slideshow, and one short video. In addition to creating new content, you need to figure out the appropriate content pieces and creative approach to scale for repackaging, recycling, and repurposing. ***Before you do any of***

that, you need to define the objectives you want to accomplish.
Although the content itself may take its own course and your
audience may use your content differently than you anticipate,
you still need to have a clear objective and target audience
in mind to plan and strategize. Holistic planning and strategic thinking about content are critical, yet we tend to spend
less time on planning and more energy on content creation
and content syndication. I will explain more about this in the
"Plan" process in Chapter 4.

In today's content-rich world, the ability
to connect different ideas and experiences is
a prerequisite for marketing. Everything else
such as planning, tools, and processes follows. Look for seemingly unrelated ideas and
patterns. Internalize how the various ideas
may or may not work for you, then custom-
ize the reworking of different ideas through
trial and error. You may not get it right the

> In today's content-rich
> world, the ability to
> connect different
> ideas and experiences
> is a prerequisite for
> marketing.

first time, but that's OK! Through your attempts and experiments, you'll discover what resonates with your audience.

In many ways, the essence of "connecting things" is what
global content marketing is all about. I am not advocating
creating something just for the sake of creating it. Connect
different experiences and ideas in a **meaningful** way, then
create something fresh, entertaining, educational, and helpful
to share with your audience. Connecting the dots also means
recognizing the geo-cultural context, which I will address
more in Chapter 1. There is no one-size-fits-all approach to
content creation and promotion. By tailoring and localizing
your content and insights, you enhance the likelihood of your
customers taking actions or changing their existing behaviors.
As a business, some key goals are to get them to try your recommendations and buy your products or services. This is by
no means easy to do. But it *is* possible, if you follow a set process. The challenges and proposed solutions for global content
marketing will be illustrated along with case studies to help
you "connect the dots." Chapter 1 highlights why global content marketing is vital. Let's get started.

CHAPTER ONE

Why Globalize Your Content

"Man—a being in search of meaning."

—PLATO

Content Marketing is Nothing New

In the United States, Costco offers the *Costco Way Cookbook* for free to its customers. I personally look forward to getting this every November. Each recipe's directions are simple to follow, and the recipes are accompanied by picturesque images of the dishes. When I flip through the cookbook, my mouth waters. There is a huge benefit to Costco for giving away this type of content to its customers. Through recipe sharing, Costco hopes to drive the sale of ingredients, which are all readily available in its warehouse stores.

Here is the beauty of the cookbook: when you look through it, you don't get a sense that Costco is trying to sell its product. The company simply provides something customers may find helpful and presents that information in a visually compelling way with high-quality print. There is no call-to-action anywhere in the cookbook to ask you to buy anything. You can buy the ingredients from Costco, but it's not necessary. This cookbook also gives an opportunity for Costco's vendors to showcase their recipes and products. You can see recipes from brands such as Krusteaz, Jimmy Dean, and the Australian Lamb Company. It provides a cobranding opportunity and another marketing channel for their vendors to showcase products. The company just shows what customers can do with ingredients if they choose to purchase from Costco. This is a perfect example of effective content marketing.

In addition to its U.S. stores, Costco also operates warehouse stores in Australia, Japan, the United Kingdom, Taiwan, Mexico, Korea, and Canada.[1] Presently, Costco doesn't offer its cookbook to other countries. This idea would also work well for international branches of Costco. A cookbook can be a great global content marketing concept because it can easily be scaled to other countries. Some U.S. recipes can apply to other Costco branches, but some recipes would need to be localized based on ingredients sold at the local Costco. Possibly the cookbook is currently not adapted to other international branches largely due to local resources and budget constraints. Or, it's simply not an effective way to drive additional sales in these local markets when compared to other marketing options. This is a classic example where one content works well for one region, but it's not adopted by others. Usually, the regional offices will make the call on what content to adapt.

This cookbook idea is not new. Betty Crocker and other food giants have done it for decades. Turn the clock back to the year 1904, and you would be reading Jell-O Corporation's cookbook. No one was familiar with the Jell-O brand at that time. Even housewives didn't know what to do with Jell-O until the company started distributing best-selling recipes and free samples that eventually contributed to sales of over $1 million by 1906.[2] In some years, as many as 15 million booklets were distributed.[3] Small pamphlets, flyers, and booklets of useful tips and information may be easily scalable across countries with translation and localization.

Let's move the clock back even further. In 1895, the *Furrow*, a free magazine published by John Deere Corporation, targeted farmers and shared agricultural and related topics for farming. It's still in print and distributed in more than 40 countries in

12 languages.[4] It's widely considered to be one of the earliest examples of content marketing by a brand and a great example of global content marketing.

We can easily continue our journey back in time and find examples of content that was published, promoted, and shared as early as the year 1040, when printing technology was first invented in China.[5] Our ancestors shared knowledge on bamboo, animal skins, or stones even before the printing press was available. Marketing the products and services through content is nothing new. Joe Pulizzi, author of Epic Content Marketing and Founder of the Content Marketing Institute, put together an infographic, *a Brief History of Content Marketing*, to share milestones of content marketing (see Figure 1.01).

FIGURE 1.01 A Brief History of Content Marketing

FIGURE 1.01 A Brief History of Content Marketing *(continued)*

Some may argue that newspapers are a form of content marketing that has been popular for centuries. As publications struggle to stay relevant today, the quality of content is critical for the success of newspapers. Because newspapers make revenue through subscriptions and advertising, I consider them to be more in the content selling business than in the content marketing business. Nevertheless, a focus on the quality of content is equally important in both content selling (media companies) and content marketing (businesses and brands).

So why does content marketing seem special now?

Everyone is Constantly Searching for Something

The mobile devices of today function as a daily planner, video player, GPS, movie theater, music player, books and more. Some of the devices even talk to us. These devices allow us to search constantly for entertainment, education, status changes, connections, or challenges. Heck, sometimes we just search mindlessly. We search for a place we crave to visit, a job we'd like to obtain, or even a skill we yearn to learn. Once that need is satisfied, we move on and search for something else. It never really stops. We search for content that will give us the best solutions, regardless of language barriers or physical boundaries.

> *We search for content that will give us the best solutions, regardless of language barriers or physical boundaries.*

My son has been playing jazz piano for years. He loves to learn new and interesting renditions. In addition to getting recommendations from his teacher on what music he should learn, he searches on YouTube for music he wants to play. Musicians around the world upload their own compositions to YouTube. Many speak a different language, yet music itself is a common language and borderless. He's discovered some interesting jazz pieces from other countries. Some musicians not only upload step-by-step instructions on how to play their compositions, they also share sheet music. My son will put his tablet on the piano and learn from the hands-on videos, even though he does not understand the languages the musicians speak. While I am still a strong believer that a teacher's face-to-face guidance and hands-on instruction are necessary if you want to master a specific skill, YouTube and other educational-based Web sites such as Open Culture, Khan Academy, and edX are a thriving breeding ground for do-it-yourself (DIY) learning.

The good news for content marketing is that demand is there, and people are searching. The bad news for content marketing is that people's attention spans are short. Depending on what information you want to communicate, you need to take into account the complexity of the topics, the length, and the format, along with your audience's needs and preferences when creating your content. You need to know your audience. You need to think like your audience.

As a marketer or a business owner creating content for multiple markets, the first step to globalizing your content is a mindset change. You need to think of your content with global usage in mind. That mindset change will determine your creative approach, translation and localization decisions, and the content formats. ***Think big on your key content pieces! Your content will be viewed by others who might not speak your language and who reside outside the local areas you serve.*** Continue to create content with a specific target audience in mind, yet think through how your creative approach, copy, or storytelling can appeal to both your target audience and audiences beyond. For small local businesses, you need to determine if global or cross-regional reach is important for the growth of your business. For some, it may not make sense. For others, the company's growth is dependent on its potential reach beyond physical locations.

> *As a marketer or a business owner creating content for multiple markets, the first step to globalizing your content is a mindset change.*

Content Creates Perception

Have you ever thought about why we go to specific Web sites on a regular basis? We all have our routines and a list of bookmarks: there are certain Web sites or aggregator apps (Reddit, Flipboard, Upworthy, Baidu, etc.) that we visit on a regular basis. We don't go there for the sake of going there, even though we are creatures of habit. The truth is, we go there to satisfy a need or multiple needs: a need to be informed, a need to be entertained, a need to be educated, a need to get help, a need to belong, a need to share, a need to brag, a need to be challenged, a need to connect, a need to disagree, a need to buy/sell something, a need to do business, and so forth. Don't we have variety of needs?

Granted, some sites satisfy our needs for talking, messaging, and shooting the breeze with each other. Most of the time we satisfy our needs by viewing, interacting, sharing, and commenting on the content on our frequently visited sites.

Content creates the perception of your brand. Perception is reality. Therefore, content should be addressed as part of your marketing strategy.

> *Content creates the perception of your brand. Perception is reality.*

For the Love of Our Devices, We Chase Content

I am part of the 75 percent, the 44 percent, and the 110 club! About 75 percent of Americans bring phones to the bathroom.[6] Approximately 44 percent of cell phone users sleep with their cell phone by their side.[7] And according to figures collected by a screen lock app, the average user actually checks his phone around 110 times a day. I've concluded that our phone is the adult version of a security blanket or our favorite stuffed animal. Marvelously, this little device does much more than act as a security blanket or substitute for a stuffed animal. It lets us consume content anytime and anywhere. Studies have shown that the typical social media user consumes 285 pieces of content daily, which equates to an eye-opening 54,000 words and, for the truly active, as many as 1,000 clickable links.[8]

When I travel to countries in Asia and Europe, I observe the same phenomena in both developed and emerging countries. Users around the world consume an enormous amount of content through their mobile devices. They may consume different content in their own or other languages, but their content consumption behaviors are very similar to ours. The content is readily available at almost no cost, aside from the cost of a data plan from a service provider. In the name of our holy phones or tablets, we all chase content! Your content, if done right, addresses your customers' needs and will be chased by your users.

Although traditional media still has its place, we no longer only "receive" information from print, radio, TV, and other traditional media outlets. More and more, people have multiple screens open when they watch TV, listen to music, or even while they work. In my household, a family of four watches TV with our tablets and phones nearby. Watching TV is no longer a passive form of "receiving" information; we can also chime in and provide real-time feedback on the programs we watch through social media platforms, consuming, researching, and discussing relevant content at the same time. We multitask to the nth degree! Our behavior has an enormous impact on content planning. We should no longer consider creating content for one screen size because our customers likely have a TV screen, phone screen, computer screen (laptop), and tablet screen open simultaneously. How can we deliver content that is seamless from one screen to another to ensure "one" experience, yet tailor different formats of content for different screen sizes? To make it more complicated, how can we scale that content with different screen sizes to different regions? Marketers' jobs seem to get tougher and tougher. Again, the ability to connect different dots in increasingly complicated and integrated marketing channels has become more urgent than ever.

> *We multitask to the nth degree! Our behavior has an enormous impact on content planning.*

Challenges and Considerations for Globalizing Content

The level of content localization and customization required for your products and services will be determined by the places and the people that you are planning to reach. Anol Bhattacharya, CEO of GetIT, wrote a blog post on B2Bento-Business-to-Business (B2B) Marketing in Asia, *Content*

Marketing Localization – Lost in Translation[9], "Language and culture are tricky things. To make sure your message is found on the other side; you need to do a lot more than just flipping words." He mentioned that there is no "United States of Asia: Asian countries have unique cultures and markets. And they are not homogeneous, like the United States, which, although a multiracial nation, largely conforms to American cultural standards." "Before you begin localizing content for a country or region, pin down what works there." It's important to recognize the internal and external challenges of scaling content globally.

Marketers' External Challenges:

- ▶ Cultural Differences
- ▶ Language Barriers
- ▶ Religious Beliefs
- ▶ Laws and Regulations
- ▶ Product Usage and Behaviors
- ▶ Marketing Promotional Channel Fragmentation

Marketers' Internal Considerations:

- ▶ Marketing Objectives
- ▶ Products and Services
- ▶ Organizational Structure and Budget Allocation
- ▶ Headquarters and Regional Collaboration
- ▶ Processes and Tools

Customers' Dilemmas:

- ▶ Information Overload
- ▶ Short Attention Span
- ▶ Decision-Making Process (Purchase Journey)
- ▶ Limited Budget

Marketers' External Challenges:

- ▶ **Cultural Differences**: People are identified with their heritage and traditions. In the United States, the ideal way to communicate is to speak directly and clearly about issues with the person involved. In Japan, the preferred way of communicating issues is to speak indirectly and artfully. A go-between person is often appointed for important matters. Another important factor to consider is how gender may affect the delivery of a message. Since there are biases in every culture that should be taken into account.

▶ **Language Barriers:** Words evoke emotion. Although English is perhaps the most dominant language in the world of business,[10] people are, in general, more apt to build emotional connections with their native language. It makes sense to add a voice-over or caption to select videos for your targeted markets to make it easier for customers in other countries. It's also important to note that British English is *not* the same as U.S. English, Indian English, or Australian English. Certain idioms that play well in one country may have very different connotations in another, even if they speak the "same" language. As Winston Churchill noted, "America and England are two nations divided by a common language."[11]

> *As Winston Churchill noted, "America and England are two nations divided by a common language."*

▶ **Religious Beliefs:** A religion's creed may dictate what and when content can be consumed. Religious beliefs are not only reflected in daily rituals, but also in festivities and seasonal celebrations. For example, Muslim New Year starts with the first day of Muharram,[12] while Chinese New Year starts on the second (occasionally the third) dark moon after the winter solstice.[13] Jewish New Year is in Tishri,[14] the seventh month of the lunar calendar, while the secular New Year in the Gregorian calendar starts in January. It's important to take into account different New Year celebrations; and it's equally important to remember how different cultures celebrate the holiday: some engage in family gatherings, others in self-reflection, or countdown to midnight. Focusing on commonalities while planning your content, marketing will minimize the need for customization.

▶ **Laws and Regulations:** Laws and regulations impact the legal disclaimers needed for the content you create. For example, the minimum legal drinking age varies dramatically around the world. To my surprise, the drinking age and purchase age are completely different in some countries. Even trickier is the age at which you can buy beer and wine versus spirits. At age 16, teenagers can buy beer and wine in Belgium and Germany, but they have to wait until the age of 18 to buy spirits.[15] Check out the legal drinking age on Wikipedia. It's a fun read. Please bear in mind that some countries don't even allow alcohol at all.[16]

▶ **Product Usage and Behaviors:** While it's common for people in Western countries to use plastic plates for quick and easy disposal, people in India and some Asian countries commonly use banana leaves as disposable plates. Once the meals are consumed, they throw away the leaves, which decompose easily. When you demonstrate your products or services in the form of a video or other formats, you need to understand how your products will be used in the local markets. B2B applications may not change much from country to country, while consumer-oriented goods may vary greatly from the package design, local ingredients, and frequency of usage to the positioning of products.

▶ **Marketing Promotional Channel Fragmentation:** Promotional channels vary from country to country or even from city to city within the same country. It depends on how the products and services are distributed and where the customers consume content. In some rural areas of India, China, and other emerging countries, mobile phone texting promotions, and door-to-door selling and leaving pamphlets behind, are still proper and fitting approaches. Yet, customers living in larger cities within India, China, and other similar countries, consume content much like customers living in metropolitan cities in the West. The rise of social media, as well as the various ways to search and shop online, has led to hyper-fragmentation of promotional channels. It adds a layer of challenge for marketers to identify effective communication methods in a myriad of fragmented marketing channels.

The rise of social media, as well as the various ways to search and shop online, has led to hyper-fragmentation of promotional channels.

Marketers' Internal Considerations:

▶ **Marketing Objectives:** Content marketing, like any other marketing function, must support both the company's business objectives and marketing objectives. Some companies may have several business objectives and a wide array of marketing objectives; you may need to prioritize your initiatives to align with limited resources and budget. Be sure to get buy-in from relevant stakeholders.

▶ **Products and Services:** Content marketing needs to provide value to customers. Of course, it's not only about selling or promoting your products and services. Some content may be educational or entertaining in nature. Hubspot is a great example. The Hubspot blog does not talk about its product offerings directly, yet the blog provides useful and educational information for marketers about inbound marketing. The company touches on topics from search engine optimization (SEO), social media, and content marketing to branding and design. It aims to provide value to prospects and progressively nurture them through useful content. This is a great example of finding a balance between creating content designed to sell and creating content designed to add value for your customers, even though it may not directly drive sales. Be able to explain to management the intent and purpose for creating content that does not directly drive sales.

▶ **Organizational Structure and Budget Allocation:** It's great when there are funds budgeted specifically for content planning and production; however, most companies do not have a specific budget line item for content. The budget for content creation may be overlooked or assumed to reside in other line items such as webmarketing, events, lead generation, advertising, and so on. From time to time, a content marketer with a limited budget may find that asking for funding from business units or other marketing departments is necessary to create additional content. For small and medium businesses (SMB), you can look for additional funding by tapping into external sources such as your customers and partners for cobranding or cocreating content. Or it may make sense to combine budget from various departments to try different formats of content with higher production cost. It's important to know which departments "own" budget and how different departments work together.

▶ **Headquarters and Regional Collaboration:** To scale content across regions, you need to set up a communication and collaboration process between headquarters and regions. Defining clear roles and responsibilities will ensure tighter integration. In some cases you may be responsible for both, headquarter and regional marketing. If that's the case, you need to make an intentional effort to understand the ins and outs of local markets and take into account localization and customization needs. Not every piece of content will work in all regions.

> *To scale content across regions, you need to set up a communication and collaboration process between headquarters and regions.*

▶ **Processes and Tools:** Global content marketing works well when there are tools and processes in place to drive cross-border content efforts such as editorial planning, content sharing, translation, syndication, measurement, and more. In my experience, processes and tools tend to be overlooked by many marketing managers. Let's take measuring the capability of content to generate leads, as an example: in order to measure the effectiveness of content marketing across regions, it's best to have the same measuring tools in place at the country level. In reality, not all the processes and tools can be deployed to all countries due to lack of language support, lack of on-site customer support, system incompatibility, and so on. You may need to implement alternate tools or even collect the data manually. Tools and processes are tricky issues, which need to be collectively discussed and communicated between headquarters and regions.

Customers' Dilemma:

While marketers face internal and external challenges, they also need to take into account their customers' needs and changing behaviors.

▶ **Information Overload:** An average of 100 hours of video is uploaded to YouTube every minute.[17] More than 190 million tweets are posted per day and 70 billion pieces of content are shared every month on Facebook.[18] A Facebook user spends an average of 15 hours and 33 minutes per month on the site, and this is in addition to other time the user may spend on other Web sites and social media networks. The amount of data people encounter on a daily basis is so overwhelming that, consciously or not, users put filters in place. Filtering creates challenges for marketers trying to get their content in front of their intended audience.

▶ **Short Attention Span:** In Nicholas Carr's post, "Is Google Making Us Stupid," he lamented the Internet chips away at his capacity for concentration and contemplation. "My mind now expects to take in information the way the Net distributes it: in a swiftly moving stream of particles."[19] In addition, the stress of modern life has reduced our attention span on a given task from 12 minutes in 1998 to 5 minutes and 7 seconds in 2008.[20] Our attention span is certainly getting shorter and shorter, which has implications for the length of content we should produce. Ekaterina Walter, co-author of *The Power of Visual Storytelling*, advocates "show, don't tell."[21] Customers have so many choices that they will exit or move on to the next piece of content if you don't catch their attention in the first five seconds.

> *Our attention span is certainly getting shorter and shorter, which has implications for the length of content we should produce.*

▶ **Decision-making Process:** Because information is produced faster than we can absorb it, the majority of us have developed a habit of skimming content without really internalizing it. Information overload, short attention spans, and habits of scanning content on the Net can paralyze our decision-making process. Sometimes I wonder how consumers make decisions at all. Given the abundance of information that is available to us at almost no cost, we should be able to make better decisions. But you could argue we make worse decisions, given the difficulty of effectively filtering out irrelevant data. This impacts how content should be presented to our customers.

▶ **Limited Budget:** Budget spending is about choice. Each day people are making decisions on how to spend their company's budget or their own money. Content marketing is about educating and influencing people before decisions are made. A customer's budget can also be impacted by tax refunds, employee bonuses, holiday seasons, and more. For content marketers, it's also important to tie specific offers or targeted content to government initiatives such as tax credits, refunds, or a major employers' bonus payout.

Content Marketing Needs to Help Your Customers Find "It"

Traveling around the oceans of the World Wide Web, people are searching for something. We are searching for what we need to know or do at the exact time we need to know or do it. The essence of content marketing is to help your customers find the information they need, in relationship to the products and services you offer. The need to be where your customers are searching has driven the boom of retargeting and contextual advertising. That form of advertising is one option to reach out to your customers. However, creating content to help, educate, support, assist, or entertain your customers is more cost-effective than an ad buy. Ad retargeting and contextual buying only lives for a limited period of time. After your ad budget is depleted, you won't be able to place new ads. Any content that provides educational and insightful value, however, can live on the Web for a long time. As a result, it creates what is known as a long tail effect, allowing different users to access your content as long as it is relevant to their needs. Generating quality content that endures over time is a big step in developing the long tail effect and is worth more than an ad buy. Make it easy for your customers to search for and purchase your products and services. By doing that, as Joe Pulizzi says, "they ultimately reward us with their business and loyalty."[22]

> Generating quality content that endures over time is a big step in developing the long tail effect and is worth more than an ad buy.

I also like the cut-to-the-chase point of view from David Meerman Scott, author of *The New Rules of Marketing and PR*: "Your customers don't care about you, your products, your services . . . they care about themselves, their wants and their needs. Content marketing is about creating interesting information your customers are passionate about so they actually pay attention to you." Scott's point is blunt and true.

In Summary

We view and interact with content more than ever before. Your content helps your customers form their perception of you and your brand. Thus, content is part of the experience you provide to your customers online and off-line. Content should be front and center of your marketing strategy, yet for most marketing professionals and senior managers, content is often an afterthought. If global content marketing is critical, how do we create a global team to align and collaborate with relevant stakeholders in the organization? What's the process of creating a successful global content marketing effort? I will discuss this in detail in Chapter 2: The 4 P's for the Global Content Marketing Process. Let's keep moving.

> *Your content helps your customers form their perception of you and your brand.*

For Entrepreneurs and Small Business Owners

- ▶ Content creates your customers' perception of your brands.
- ▶ Be there to help, educate, support, and assist. Make it easy for your customers.
- ▶ Invest in processes and tools to track results.

For Enterprise Marketing Managers

- ▶ Content creates your customers' perception of your brands.
- ▶ Integrate content marketing as part of an overall marketing strategy.
- ▶ Set up a communication and collaboration process between the headquarters and local teams.

For Agencies and Marketing Consultants

► Connecting different ideas and experiences is a prerequisite for marketing. Help your customers connect the dots they don't see.

► Assist your customers in understanding the internal and external challenges of global content marketing.

► Recommend the appropriate tools and processes for your customers.

CHAPTER TWO

What Are the 4 P's of the Global Content Marketing Cycle?

"The 4 P's of Marketing: Please, Please, Please, Please."

—SHREYAS NAVARE[1]

The Original 4 P's of Marketing

I chuckle when I see this quote from Shreyas Navare. Everyone who has studied marketing in the past 50 years has been introduced to the 4 P's of marketing. In 1960,[2] E. Jerome McCarthy, an American marketing professor and the author of the influential book *Basic Marketing: A Managerial Approach*, presented the four elements of marketing, which have served as the basis of marketing for the past century. These four elements are Product, Price, Place and Promotion.

▶ **Product:** Create a desirable product or a unique service to satisfy the needs of your customer. Define it in terms of what it does for your customers. Product name, design, packaging, features, and benefits will reinforce the positioning, target audience, and industries.

▶ **Price:** Set an optimal price structure, balancing the needs of your company and the desires of your customers. Pricing has a profound impact on marketing strategy and positioning.

▶ **Place:** Offer your products and services at places that are convenient for your customers to access. This P not only includes your business models such as direct sales, use of resellers, direct mail, retailers, and so on, but it also refers to the logistics for the delivery of services or physical product. These decisions will have an impact on your overall marketing strategy.

▶ **Promotion:** Communicate to inform your audience about the benefits of your products, the way to buy, and the pricing. There are various promotional tactics associated with different marketing communications channels such as public relations (PR), advertising, TV, print, online, and more. Facilitate the purchase journey from the first point of contact to the completion of sales.

The 4 P's of marketing are the core concepts for creating the right product at the right price in the right place with effective promotion.

In summary, the 4 P's of marketing are the core concepts for creating the right product at the right price in the right place with effective promotion. The 4 P's have morphed into 5 P's to include People involved in your marketing efforts.

The 4 C's of Consumer Marketing

In the 1990's,[3] Robert Lauterborn introduced the 4 C's as new definitions for the four P's. His model shifts the focus from the producer to the consumer. In the traditional marketing model, we sold what we made or produced. In the new marketing model, we need to sell what customers want. These C's reflect a more consumer-oriented marketing approach.

▶ **Consumer** (versus Product): Study consumers' wants and needs. Create products tailored to these desires and needs.

- ► **Cost** (versus Price): Reflect the reality of total cost. If you sell a computer, the cost of searching or driving to a retail store to purchase it should be taken into account.
- ► **Convenience** (versus Place): Understand your customer's preferred method of purchase—on the Internet, at a store, by phone, from a catalogue, or other ways.
- ► **Communication** (versus Promotion): Focus on communications between customers and businesses. It's broader than just promotion. Communication is as much about listening as it is about talking.

The 4 P's of Business-to-Business Marketing

In 2013, Richard Ettenson, Eduardo Conrado, and Jonathan Knowles published an article in the *Harvard Business Review*, "Rethinking the 4 P's" for Business-to-Business (B2B).[4] "In a five-year study involving more than 500 managers and customers in multiple countries" they discovered the original 4 P's model does not fully apply to B2B marketing. The 4 P's are still relevant, but need to be interpreted differently.

- ► **Solution** (versus Product): Provide solutions to solve your customer's issues and challenges, not by product features and functions.
- ► **Value** (versus Price): Articulate the benefit relative to price rather than how price relates to production cost and profit margins.
- ► **Access** (versus Place): Focus on cross-channel presence that considers the customers' purchase journey instead of focusing on individual purchase locations.
- ► **Education** (versus Promotion): Provide information relevant to customers' needs in the purchase cycle.

From the original 4 P's to the 4 C's and then rethinking the 4 P's, different interpretations have been applied to Product, Price, Place, and Promotion. The essence does not change: create desirable products

The essence does not change: create desirable products and services to meet the needs of customers. Provide relevant information at the time needed.

and services to meet the needs of customers. Provide relevant information at the time needed.

The 4 P's of the Global Content Marketing Cycle

In the context of this book, there are 4 P's to creating a successful global content marketing effort. This model of 4 P's focuses on the stages of building a global content marketing plan that connects business with customers: Plan, Produce, Promote and Perfect (see Figure 2.02).

> *This model of 4 P's focuses on the stages of building a global content marketing plan that connects business with customers: Plan, Produce, Promote and Perfect.*

Plan: Strategy before execution

Collaborate with relevant stakeholders on regional and country teams to create a global content marketing strategy that aligns target audiences, key success metrics, priority countries, and strategic editorial topics with your business objectives. Alignment of objectives and strategy is vital because it dictates content creation, promotion and measurement.

Produce: Create content that matters

Develop relevant stories that meet identified countries' needs with different formats based on strategic editorial topics that address the target audience's pain points, desires, and challenges. Use tools and data to optimize continuous content production.

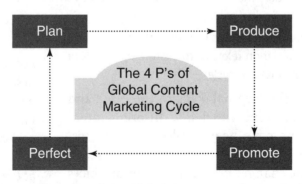

FIGURE 2.01 The 4 P's of the Global Content Marketing Cycle

Promote: Distribute content in the digital era

Establish a market-driven content distribution process with paid and social media. Publish the appropriate formats of content with the optimal frequency in targeted channels. Use tools and data to optimize the media buy and social media content distribution.

Perfect: Measure and optimize to drive the maximum impact

Continuously optimize and measure the impact of content marketing as part of an ongoing feedback loop. Define goals and use tools and processes to maximize the effectiveness of content production and content syndication. To improve the previous 3 P's: Plan, Produce and Promote.

Let's Define Headquarters versus Local

A couple of terms will keep coming up throughout this book. The head office, corporate, and headquarters are used interchangeably. The headquarters isn't necessarily the main office. It's a group of people with organization-wide responsibilities, not focusing on specific local markets. Corporate persons can also reside in the local markets, but they are responsible for organization-wide activities. The headquarters marketing department is the corporate (central) marketing organization that sets marketing strategies, provides guidance, processes, and tools to market products and services. In smaller companies, marketing may wear both hats of managing organization-wide and local market responsibilities.

"Local" refers to regions or countries where the company has a local presence. Local presence does not necessarily mean the company has a physical office in each local country. To be efficient and save money, some companies choose to handle an entire region out of a single central office, but regional marketing will assess each local market differently. Regions and countries are also terms used frequently in this book. In technology companies or multinational companies (MNCs), terms such as *geographies* or *geos* are also used to describe the region or country teams. Some of you may be familiar with EMEA (Europe, the Middle East, and Africa) as the pan-Europe, the Middle East, and Africa regions; APAC as pan-Asia Pacific regions; and Americas covering North, Central, and South America regions. This is a book about the process of the headquarters and local teams working together to achieve corporate goals.

Going forward, I will first discuss how to organize a team so that it is set up for successful global content marketing in the subsequent chapter. Then, after diving into the 4 P's in detail, I will dig into what the 3 A's and 3 C's are all about and what servant leadership has to do with the formation of a global team. In addition to it, I will also share an extended list of topics to drive conversations between the corporate and local teams. So, lets read on!!

CHAPTER THREE

Organize a Team for Global Content Marketing Success

"If everyone is moving forward together, then success takes care of itself."

—HENRY FORD[1]

This quote from Henry Ford describes the essence of global marketing. No global marketing effort is impromptu or spontaneous. It usually requires extensive collaboration and coordination between headquarters and regions, regardless of the size of a company. Well-intentioned efforts ensure that people in both headquarters and regions are moving in the same direction and striving to achieve the same goals. Ford had another quote on working together as one team that I also like very much: "Coming together is a beginning, staying together is progress, and working together is success."[2] A global content plan is a means to get everyone to come together, which is a great beginning.

> No global marketing effort is impromptu or spontaneous. It usually requires extensive collaboration and coordination.

I will discuss how to create a global content plan collectively in Chapter 4. The next step of "staying together" and "working together" through thick and thin needs to be accomplished through processes, tools, and regular communications in order to move global content marketing efforts forward (see Figure 3.01).

To pull a global content team together, we need to start by answering these questions:

▶ Given the goals of the global content marketing effort, who are the right people for the team?

▶ What are the appropriate processes to stay in sync and be productive as a team?

▶ Which tools are most appropriate for global content marketing collaboration?

▶ What are the rules to drive decisions, if we can't satisfy all regions' needs and requests?

FIGURE 3.01 A global content marketing success is the combination of coming together and working together, then staying together through the 4 P's stages of the content marketing cycle.

Build the Team with 3 A's and 3 C's

There are 3 A's for the team to come together and 3 C's for the team to work together. The 3 A's and 3 C's serve as a foundation for the team to stay together through the stages of the Global Content Marketing Cycle: Plan, Produce, Promote, and Perfect.

- ▶ 3 A's—Come together as a team:
  - ▶ **Align** on objectives and goals
  - ▶ **Assemble** the team
  - ▶ **Act** with clear roles and responsibilities
- ▶ 3 C's—Work together as a team:
  - ▶ **Collaborate** with a set of commonly used tools and processes
  - ▶ **Communicate** through regular sync meetings between headquarters and regions
  - ▶ **Compromise** by making hard calls without hard feelings

The 3 A's and the 3 C's are essential to move the team along through the 4 P's stages of the global content marketing cycle.

The 3 A's for Coming Together

I often feel that pulling a team together for content marketing is like Chris' (played by Yul Brynner) journey of finding the other six men in *The Magnificent Seven*. Chris' mission is to protect a poor village raided by a gang led by Calvera (played by Eli Wallach). He tried to convince the other six to join him for the battle despite being outnumbered, with only a slim chance of winning. But he clearly understood what he wanted to accomplish and assembled a team by appealing to aspects of the venture that resonated emotionally with each participant.

Like Chris, before assembling your team, you need to understand why you want to assemble a team, what you want to accomplish as a team, and why it's in the best interests of

> *Your global content marketing mission may not be as heroic as that of "The Magnificent Seven" but you will likely have fewer casualties.*

prospective team members to participate. The process of coming together starts with sharing objectives, finding players, and acting as a team. Your global content marketing mission may not be as heroic as that of *"The Magnificent Seven"* but you will likely have fewer casualties. Your additional goal is to achieve your marketing and business objectives by creating a win–win situation for headquarters, local teams, and your customers.

▶ Align: Share objectives and goals
▶ Assemble: Pull the right team together
▶ Act: Identify roles and responsibilities

The first A: Align Objectives and Goals

Let's define objective and strategy first. Objective is "what do you want to accomplish?" Strategy is "how do you accomplish your objectives?" As a global team, you must align "what" with strategic guidance on "how" from the very beginning of planning. For example: The business objective is to grow revenue by 15%. One of the marketing objectives is to build awareness and preference of a specific product with a specific set of target audience. One of the marketing strategies may be to build awareness of a specific product by enabling sales teams and running integrated campaigns. The specifics of how to enable sales teams and what types of campaigns to run will vary from country to country. The "specifics" of how tend to be called "tactics" by the team at headquarters, but it's referred to as "regional or country strategy" by the regional and country teams. Don't get stuck on that as long as the headquarters and local teams agree on marketing objectives and high-level strategic guidance. Understanding your company's business and marketing objectives is absolutely essential. What drives your company's business? Are the goals geared toward content marketing, online sales, subscriptions, leads, app downloads, or referrals? Which countries are priorities for growth?

How does content play a role in the context of your business model and marketing communications?

In a big enterprise, we may not have control over the entire sales and marketing process. The roles and responsibilities are narrowly defined across multiple marketing functions, business units, and various countries. Our content marketing efforts are likely confined to only a single step in the value chain. However, it's different for small- and medium-sized businesses (SMBs); because people tend to wear multiple hats, a larger scope is covered by a smaller team. Our goal is to focus on those processes that we can control and keep the regional priorities in mind when it comes to alignment between the headquarters and regions.

We Are on the Same Page, but I Need Different Content

Although regions may be aligned on objectives and high-level guidance on strategy, the detailed local strategies (which some may refer to as tactics) may drive different content requirements. Here is a great example: Headquarters' objective is to "grow revenue by expanding the healthcare segment." Regardless of whether you are located in headquarters or countries, we all understand that's our business objective. Given that many hospitals are state-owned in China, to expand into the healthcare segment is to influence the healthcare officials of the federal and state governments who will specify the key technologies, systems, and devices that hospitals will buy. The local marketing team's objective aligns with the corporate objective, yet it requires a marketing strategy different from other regions: "Grow revenue by influencing the healthcare officials in the central and local governments to select our products."

On the surface, the country's objective aligns with the corporate business strategy, which is to drive growth in the healthcare segment. But that slight change of influencing healthcare officials has a huge impact on content planning. Based on the corporate business objective, the target audiences would seem to be doctors and hospital administrators. By reading the country's strategy, the target audience is changed to government healthcare officials. Doctors, hospital administrators, and healthcare officials may require similar information and care about similar topics, but they may not prefer the same content formats or visit the same sites to find information. This slight change in a country's business strategy has a big impact on content creation and media promotional plans.

The Chinese objective is very much aligned with the corporate objective, but its content requirements are suddenly different. As a headquarters representative, how do you deal with that? As an affiliate located in the region, how do you work with headquarters to voice your concerns and requests, given that your target audience has deviated from corporate's recommended audience? As an agency person, will this piece of information impact your content deliverables? Can you help your client connect more dots and be more efficient?

Headquarters has several options to address the audience change request and content needs:

▶ Let the region take the lead: The Chinese marketing team sets the direction and takes care of their content needs by focusing on healthcare government officials using their own budget and resources.

▶ Let the region take the lead, but with headquarters allocating budget for localization:

   ▶ Work together with the region to review the list of global content and identify a short list of pieces that will work for their audiences.

   ▶ Allocate budget so regions can take the lead in localizing and translating selected content as necessary.

▶ Headquarters takes the lead to provide full geographical support: Acknowledge this is a new audience that headquarters needs to support and ensure the content roadmap will include content pieces targeted to healthcare government officials. Budget and resources will be allocated accordingly.

Depending on headquarters' decision, the Chinese marketing team can determine what it want to do next. Then, corporate and the Chinese marketing team can reach an agreement on how to best approach content planning to support the Chinese market's needs.

The Second A: Assemble Your Team

Once you agree on objectives and strategies, you need to pull together the right players. Building global content marketing's success requires a cohesive team that is willing to put in the time (late nights or early mornings to accommodate time zone differences) and effort (localization and translation). No successful global effort is random or unstructured. Foremost, you need to bring together a group of core players and help set the direction needed to drive mutually desired content marketing efforts. Who are the players that you should invite to drive the global content marketing effort? It depends on what you want to accomplish.

> *Building global content marketing's success requires a cohesive team that is willing to put in the time.*

Depending on the aspect of global content marketing you work on, very likely you will work with different groups of people. Regardless of the size of a company, you may work with one group to create a global content plan, yet work with a slightly different group for content creation, depending on topics and products. Then, it's another group of people who deliver measurements and reports, which will depend on the mix of marketing channels such as the company Web site, paid media, social media, print, and other media. Adding to the complexity of assembling your team, some content-related activities are outsourced; you will probably need to invite agencies or independent contractors to be part of the team to support cross-regional content efforts. What you want to accomplish will determine the right players to pull together.

Finding the Usual Suspects Is Unusual

Getting a group of the right players for global content marking may not be as easy as you think, especially if you work for a big global enterprise. For a big enterprise, each person has a more specialized or narrowly defined role. Additionally, the titles don't always tell us much about their real jobs. A lot of them have a generic title such as "marketing manager" or "marketing specialists." I have known content producers with titles such as creative services manager, product marketing manager, content manager, sales enablement training manager, sales operations manager, digital marketing manager or even evangelist. You need to inquire diligently into other people's tribal knowledge to know who's who at both the global and local levels for content marketing.

> *Inquire diligently into other people's tribal knowledge to know who's who at both the global and local levels for content marketing.*

Is it easier for a smaller company to find out who is doing what? Not really! While employees in a big enterprise have specialized or specific roles, the opposite holds true for smaller companies, where one person may wear multiple hats. So, the same rule applies: you still need to inquire diligently into other people's tribal knowledge to know who's who at both the global and local levels for content marketing. Although the same solution applies, the scope of engagement and the formality of communications vary from enterprises to small businesses. While discovering who's who, you will also realize some roles are missing, and you need to determine how to close the gap either by hiring external (i.e., an agency) help, doing some of it yourself, or asking other team members to cover.

Here is a partial list of relevant content marketing players. Again, the titles and roles may differ from company to company and from industry to industry:

- ▶ Editor/Editor-in-Chief
- ▶ Content Strategist
- ▶ Content Creator/Content Manager
- ▶ Product Marketing Manager
- ▶ Brand Manager
- ▶ Media Manager
- ▶ Legal
- ▶ Social Media Manager/Community Manager

- ▶ Webmaster
- ▶ Sales Operations Managers /Marketing Operations Managers
- ▶ PR
- ▶ Copywriter/Writer
- ▶ Graphic Designer
- ▶ Region or Country Marketing Manager
- ▶ SEO Manager (Search Engine Optimization)
- ▶ SEM Manager (Search Engine Marketing)
- ▶ Direct Marketing Manager
- ▶ IT (Information Technology) Marketing Support
- ▶ Agency

Editor/Editor-in-Chief: This role is common in publishing or media companies. This is not a typical role seen in traditional enterprises or small businesses. Some companies that are very savvy in content marketing or social media communications have roles similar to editorial functions, but they may not call them editors. In some organizations, it can be writers who also wear editors' hats. Some editors oversee multichannel editorial, some focus on a single channel such as social media, community, or other venues. At a more tactical level, the editorial functions reside with the social media manager or media manager. Some editorial functions reside with marketing managers who create go-to-market plans at a more strategic level. In some companies, editorial duties are parsed out to different marketing functions, which are responsible for outbound communication such as e-mail campaigns, events, and the like. For example, if you manage online communities and corporate blogs, you have your own editorial calendar. If you manage social media, you likely also have your own editorial calendar. You need to understand how or if editorial planning is done at both the strategic and tactical levels and who may be performing the editorial function in your company.

Content Strategist: Dan Zambonini, Director of Box UK, published a great blog post on Contentini entitled "Content Strategists: What Do They Do?" There can be some overlap between content strategists and editors-in-chief. While editors-in-chief may focus on the overall editorial planning and content creation, content strategists cover the entire content cycle from strategizing, analyzing, producing, publishing, and monitoring content. Furthermore, "information architecture, delivery technologies, and anything else that affects the impact of content falls under the purview of the conscientious content strategist."[3] With this definition in mind, a content strategist's role can be broader than editor-in-chief. Again, not every company has a content strategist, yet I have seen this function hidden and grouped with other responsibilities, such as digital marketing or social media marketing, e-mail marketing, or other marketing functions. If a content strategist's role exists in a company, this person tends to lead the global content marketing effort.

Content Creator/Content Manager: These people are known as messaging managers, copywriters, digital marketing managers, creative services managers, or video editors, among other titles. Some specialize in specific formats of content production; some are jacks-of-all-trades. Again, they may be hidden or grouped within different roles.

Product Marketing Manager: This role tends to reside within business units or product groups. The product marketing manager can also be the subject matter experts on products or technologies. They are great sources for providing product-related information. Some product marketing managers also write for technical training or sales collateral, so they can also be considered content creators.

Brand Manager: Most brand managers are responsible for company or brand development such as product naming and logo development, company branding style guides, or even creative development. However, at some companies, brand managers are responsible for P & L (profit and loss) of specific product brands. They oversee the brand's overall marketing efforts from strategy setting to campaign executions.

Media Manager: People who are responsible for media planning and buying, advertising, media and event sponsorship, advertorials and customized programs with media partners. They need someone to help them understand what content is available for production promotion and content syndication for paid-media effort.

Legal: Content marketing's "BFF." Any content that has definite claims that can possibly be questioned will need a blessing from the legal department.

Social Media Manager/Community Manager: Social media managers are responsible for the company's presence on social media platforms such as Facebook, Twitter, Weibo (Chinese version of Twitter), VKontakte (Russian version of Facebook), and others. Some social media managers focus on ramping social media tools and setting up compliance, which may not directly relate to content marketing. In some companies, community managers are also social media managers. Community managers who monitor and maintain online communities have a great vested interest in global content efforts and need to understand what content is coming through the pipeline so they can plan and fill the community's editorial calendar to drive interaction and engagement with their community members.

Webmaster: They can also be called web producers, digital marketing managers, or content managers in some companies. Webmasters are responsible for the design and maintenance of the company's Web site and communities. With content updated regularly, they need to understand when pages need to be refreshed, as well as what and when new content will be available.

Sales Operations Manager/Marketing Operations Manager: In some companies, content-related tools selection and sourcing resides with the sales or marketing operations team. Some sales operations are also responsible for sales enablement and sales training. By working closely with IT, some marketing operations are responsible for content tool selection, process implementation and marketing infrastructure deployment.

Public Relations (PR): Public relations also called PR, does not only issue media releases and stage media events but also creates key messages, press articles, and editorials to communicate with the media and press.

Copywriter/Writer: People responsible for the text in content creation. They tend to be generalists. They need to be briefed properly to create content or localize content for regions.

Graphic Designer: All visual elements of content and its overall "look-and-feel" falls to the graphic designer. To create global content, this role needs to understand cultural sensitivities to ensure that graphic elements are transferable across regions.

Region or Country Marketing Manager: Some roles expand into regions and require an in-depth local and regional knowledge. Depending on the company and functions, all the roles mentioned previously can have similar functions in regions and countries.

SEO Manager: An SEO manager is responsible for organic search of Web pages. This role can be at the headquarters or the local level.

SEM Manager: An SEM manager is responsible for paid search and keyword buys. This role can be centralized to coordinate keyword buys.

Direct Marketing Manager: A direct marketing manager handles online and off-line direct marketing efforts. This role can also be a demand generation manager.

Event Marketing Manager: This manager is responsible for tradeshows, industry events, exhibits, and event sponsorship executions.

IT Marketing Support: This is another Best Friend Forever (BFF) for content marketers. The IT team plays an important role to ensure tools and platforms are integrated and work together. Having IT's input and participation is necessary at times, and making sure IT understands your needs enables them to adequately prepare the appropriate infrastructure and technology solutions.

Agency: Some companies, especially SMBs, outsource most of their content-marketing-related responsibilities to agencies and freelancers. Agencies can also provide all of the defined roles in a team with experience.

The challenge in pulling together a team is that titles and job responsibilities don't usually align. It's even blurrier in the modern marketing world with the emergence of social media and company Web site management. Many jobs for social media have been created without industry-recognizable titles. To assemble your team, you need to know who does what. Most important, *you must know what you want to accomplish first*. Your goals will determine who the right players for your team are. Different teams need to be assembled at different stages of the content marketing cycle. Knowing who's who and being able to plug and play is critical to moving things forward. I will discuss this further in one of the 3 C's, "Collaborate." Another compass to help you assemble your team is your global content plan, which I will discuss later in Chapter 4.

To make things even more complicated people move around, companies go through reorganizations, and the budget fluctuates. Your dream team may change like the four seasons. That's OK! Change is the only constant in life. So, how do we deal with people changes to make sure it does not slow down your global content effort?

The Third A: Act Together with Clear Roles and Responsibilities

Once you assemble a team that is aligned to the content marketing objectives, the next step is to define crisp roles and responsibilities for a cohesive team. In a global collaboration, it's important to understand the collaboration model and the communications approach. Simply put, it's who owns what and who leads what. Here is a simple question: Who owns content creation? Very likely both the headquarters and regions will say that they own it. But that creates confusion over dual ownership. Then, the next question is who should lead? If the product or services are highly

> It's important to understand the collaboration model and the communications approach. Simply put, it's who owns what and who leads what.

localized, it makes sense for regions or countries to lead the content creation effort, but have headquarters provide style guides and a creative playbook so that regions and countries can create content with a consistent look and feel. Let's face it: in the real world, nothing is ever 100% clear. This is especially true when many people are involved and deadlines loom. Make an effort to define roles as clearly as possible to help minimize confusion between the headquarters and regions.

The Tug of War: Headquarters versus Local

Here is the reality: The tension of headquarters versus local occurs in every discipline of a company that sells and markets products cross regionally. The power and responsibilities move from the center to the edge, then back again, depending on a myriad of factors such as organizational structure, funding allocation, or managerial directions at any given time. Headquarters is frustrated that a region's executions are not on brand or on strategy; the regions are annoyed that headquarters is moving too slowly or providing messaging and content that doesn't resonate with local audiences. For content planning and collaboration, there is always discussion between headquarters and regions on who does what or who owns what. That tension will never go away, so the task is to understand what to centralize and decentralize, who takes the lead and who follows. To make decisions on who owns what, here are some elements that you should take into account to determine centralization versus decentralization:

The tension of headquarters versus local occurs in every discipline of a company that sells and markets products cross regionally.

- ▶ Products
- ▶ Organizational Structure
- ▶ Budget Allocation
- ▶ Corporate Culture

▶ Management Preference

▶ Company Politics

Products: If products are highly localized, like the McDonald's menus in India and the United States, it makes sense for content creation and production to reside within country. In this scenario, India has a huge population of vegetarians. Content created in the United States may focus on healthy eating and calorie counts, while content in India may focus on promoting a wide array of vegetarian choices (McVeggie, Veg Pizza, McPuff, Veg Supreme, etc.). Headquarters will focus on providing strategy, sales goals, high-level messaging and/or positioning, creative guidance, and budget allocation. Local teams focus on execution and implementation.

Organizational Structure: Some companies' corporate offices are lean and mean, and they choose to allocate more head count resources to countries. In this case, the regions and countries may take on more responsibility and ownership for scaling or creating content.

Budget: Money means power. Where the budget resides plays a critical role. If budget resides with corporate, which in turn allocates to the regional level, then headquarters has more authority over locals. If the budget resides within countries, local offices usually have more autonomy.

Corporate Culture: Some corporate offices offer full autonomy to regions as long as they meet P & L goals. Some head offices prefer tighter marketing and creative control over local marketing efforts.

Management Preference: In some companies, the VP of Sales or the CMO can single-handedly determine how to strike a balance between corporate and local.

Company Politics: Sometimes the biggest obstacles to collaborative efforts are departmental silos, territorialism, and noncooperation. For example, a direct marketing department only cares about lead generation content and insists on creating only product-specific content.

Understanding these internal factors will help you gauge the corporate landscape and determine the right model of decentralization versus centralization needed to mitigate tension up front. Here are a couple examples of decentralization versus centralization:

SEM: Headquarters leads by centrally determining and recommending the list of keywords and the keyword buy for specific editorial topics and cross-regional campaigns. If you have an SEM agency, they can run the translation of keywords for regions and countries to review. Regions and countries have the right to review and approve the keywords. Even if there is no SEM agency to manage SEM or keyword translation for some companies, a list of recommended keywords should still come from headquarters as a baseline for the region and countries team to translate and localize. Then, the local teams can manage the keyword ad buy locally for their campaigns.

Cross-Regional Events or Road Shows: It can be more effective if the headquarters event team leads the theme creation, creative/style guide, messaging and promotional templates, keynotes, and sponsorship sales of the events, leaving the regions and countries to focus on event production, attendee acquisition, on-the-ground promotion, and training sessions.

This is the same for global content planning. Headquarters leads content strategy, annual and quarterly editorial planning, product messaging, and a list of content deliverables, while regions and countries lead localization, customization, marketing campaigns, event training, and content distribution.

The balancing of centralization versus decentralization can reflect the tug-of-war between the corporate and local offices. The general rule is that anything cross regional is more effective when led by headquarters. Innovations are welcome from both headquarters and local teams. Dell's 2008 Take Your Own Path (TYOP) campaign, which targeted SMBs, was initiated by their Asia-Pacific marketing team.[4] Dell's headquarters loved the concept and worked with the regional marketing teams to scale to countries such as the United States, the United Kingdom, Japan, Germany, and China.[5]

Headquarters' Role: To Lead Is to Serve

The beginning of a beautiful relationship in global content marketing: headquarters is here to lead and serve.

> *The beginning of a beautiful relationship in global content marketing: headquarters is here to lead and serve.*

Working in a global role at headquarters for over 15 years, I have maintained fairly good relationships with all my geographical counterparts. No matter how confrontational the situation was, we were able to find a solution. I attribute the success of our partnership to one important factor: headquarters' role is to serve. This echoes Robert K. Greenleaf's 1970 essay, "The Servant as Leader." He also coined the term, Servant Leadership.[6] I see myself as a *support* person to my geographical counterparts. I am here to make them successful, and that includes providing leadership and clear guidance, finding budget, and offering help whenever possible. Leadership is part of the service: providing clear directions to regions so they can create plans to accomplish the corporation's objectives and goals. At the same time, it's important to let regions know that headquarters supports them.

Which Is It? Stay Out of the Way or Tell Them What to Do?

I also believe that to lead is not to tell geographies what to do. To lead is to provide guidance so geographies can execute with a certain level of autonomy. I have been lucky to work with very competent regional marketing managers for a long time. I tend to stay out of their way. By having conversations with other industry peers and marketing managers in start-ups, I discovered that sometimes it's necessary to provide your regions with specific directions. The depth of headquarters' engagement with regions depends on:

- ▶ A region or country's experience level
- ▶ The trust and working relationship between headquarters and geographies
- ▶ Past marketing results

The correct path has a great deal to do with the maturity of a company or the regions. Maybe the regions are expanding too quickly and they just don't have enough resources and budget to do everything. In that case, tell them what to prioritize. Perhaps the regional marketing managers are new; you need to give them specific directions so that they can quickly make progress. You may need to adjust your communications and support models based on your assessments of geographical capabilities and competency. This may also include giving regions specific directions on what to do and how to do it. If you are actively involved in the details of the executions, please make sure you can defend your decisions with reasons, logic, or data.

The opposite can be true too: Geographies may understand their local markets and corporate processes so well that they are telling headquarters what to do and what they need. This can be true when headquarters is not in the leadership position and the regions that own budget and sales quota are taking the lead. Ultimately, the team needs to be built on trust. We trust that we are one team and we work for the same company (sadly, not everyone understands that). It also helps when compensation is at least partly based on overall corporate goals and profitability and not just on individual or divisional targets. To build one team is to assemble the right players, share the same vision, align on the same goals, and act with a sense of trust and clearly defined roles.

Ultimately, the team needs to be built on trust. We trust that we are one team and we work for the same company (sadly, not everyone understands that).

The 3 C's for Staying Together

After coming together, we need to stay together throughout the journey. I often joke that staying together as a global team is like maintaining the relationship of a married couple who don't live together, but see each other once a quarter and talks to each other on a regular basis on the phone or through video conferencing. The process to keep the relationship going is regular communication to drive resolutions.

- ▶ Collaborate: Cooperate and agree on plans, processes, and tools to achieve win–win situations.
- ▶ Communicate: Set up a regular schedule to have open and honest discussions and proactively identify and resolve issues.
- ▶ Compromise: Make hard calls on priorities collectively.

The First C: Collaborate

I am often asked what tools and processes are needed to drive global content marketing collaboration. It depends on what you want to solve and accomplish. I recommend you sit back and evaluate which stage of the 4 P's you are in and what you want to accomplish at that stage.

Plan is about business goal alignment, content strategy, audience identification, and editorial planning. Produce is about content brainstorming, creation using various formats, and collaboration with various authors and approvers in a structured workflow. Promote is about content distribution and syndication. Finally, Perfect is about content measurement and optimization. Each stage requires a set of processes and tools to collaborate. Using Produce as an example, you will need a workflow to brainstorm, review, and create content. You may also need a tool to help you track the progress of various content pieces. There is no one mighty tool that will cover issues for all four stages. Very likely you will need to have different tools for different purposes.

In general, there are hundreds of content management software applications out there. Some content management tools are specifically tailored for Web site management, some are more appropriate for content production. Some focus on content distribution to social media platforms with a set of measurements. You need to understand your requirements for the tools and then determine which ones work for you. The Content Marketing Tools Ultimate List that follows is not a comprehensive list, but it maps the content marketing challenges along with potential content marketing tools (see Figure 3.02).

> *Cross-regional collaboration and communication will only work if the tools are in place and easy to use.*

Cross-regional collaboration and communication will only work if the tools are in place and easy to use. Technology enables and improves the efficiency of your content marketing effort.

There are several fundamental tools, which are necessary to drive content marketing efforts in a company:

► Content publishing tools for social media platforms
► Content management software
► Marketing automation tools
► Customer relationship management (CRM)
► Web platform(s)

If you would like to monitor the inbound traffic on your Web site from outbound marketing communications, it's important to have your content publishing tools and content management software integrated with marketing automation and your customer relationship management systems. In reality, the systems tend to be siloed and not all the systems are available across all countries.

To globalize tools and processes is a challenge for marketers. From my experience, tools tend to lag behind plans and execution. We tend to focus on getting campaigns running or launching products first, while the tools setup tends to happen either in the midst of everything or as an afterthought. Interestingly, while talking to some of my industry peers, they see the opposite: they consider the tools so critical that they are part of the up-front planning for a campaign.

Those at headquarters should always think about tools with a global perspective in mind, if possible. Not every tool used by headquarters will work or be available in other countries and vice versa. The goals and selection criteria of any tool should incorporate geographies' feedback; yet, the potential downside of thinking with global marketing in mind is the cost and customization of each tool. Also, it can be expensive to launch

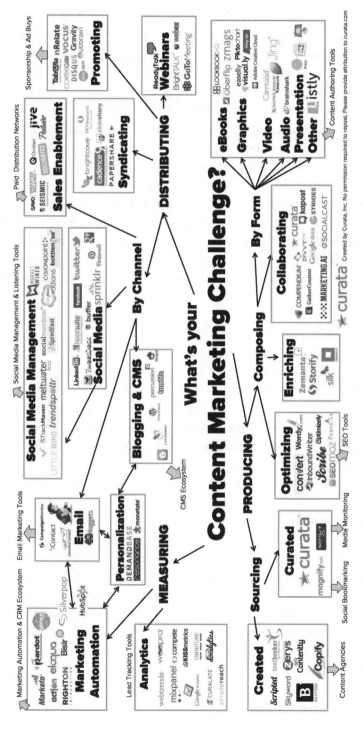

FIGURE 3.02 The Content Marketing Tools Ultimate List[7]

new global tools. Due to the cost and pressing timelines, it may make sense to have regions source local tools first. In addition to the budget discussion, back-end tools and processes take as much discussion and compromise as creative development. It's boring and dull, but tool discussions should be a standing topic for regular headquarters and local sync meetings.

For a smaller company, collaboration can be achieved simply by making a call or meeting ad hoc, yet processes and tools are still needed to drive cross-regional collaboration. It's not different from large enterprises in that respect.

This is the same for global content planning. Headquarters can be responsible for content strategy, annual and quarterly editorial planning, product messaging, and a list of content deliverables, while the geographies focus on localization, customization, marketing campaigns, training, and content distribution.

The Second C: Communicate

When it comes to a successful global team, there is no such thing as overcommunicating.

When it comes to a successful global team, there is no such thing as overcommunicating. There are always people in different countries who, not that are not in the loop on the latest changes or content plan updates. The trick is to find a good time to meet and the right tools to facilitate communication. But when is the right time to meet? There is really no right or wrong answer; you need to find a time that works for you and your teams.

I have facilitated a recurring global meeting that has participants from all regions. I set that meeting at 11:00 p.m. EST (Eastern Standard Time) to accommodate all regions' schedules. No matter what time you select, you will still have someone calling in at night or during dinner or lunch. A suggestion is to alternate the time periodically so that no one region or country gets stuck with always attending at a suboptimal time.

Another option is to run two separate headquarter/regions sync calls with the same agenda. One is scheduled at 10:00 or 11:00 a.m. EST with North America, Latin America, Europe, the Middle East, and Africa. The other one is scheduled at 8:00 p.m. or 9:00 p.m. EST with Asia Pacific. Unfortunately, this is not ideal for teams who are based in India. However, having two separate calls with the same agenda has worked well for me at times.

It's important that headquarters "leads" the meeting, publishes the agenda, and follows-up on action items. As I mentioned earlier, headquarters' job is to lead and to serve.

Having a regular meeting with published minutes is not enough. There is always someone who is on vacation or has a conflict and can't attend the meetings. I also find that a monthly newsletter and e-mail to share the global content marketing effort is helpful to keep the broader team in the loop.

> *A monthly newsletter and e-mail to share the global content marketing effort is helpful to keep the broader team in the loop.*

The Third C: Compromise

When you have the right players in place and meet on a regular basis, every geography has its content wish list they would like to accomplish and for which they wish to receive headquarters' support. With limited budget and resources, it's important to prioritize. Headquarters can't make everyone happy. Sometimes, it's important to make hard decisions and say "No" to select regions and countries. Conversely regions and countries may need to say "No" to headquarters on editorial and content recommendations. Saying "No" is not hard if you can explain your decision with logic and reason. When evaluating the priorities, it's important to tie back to the business objectives and goals. Ask again and again: What do we want to accomplish? How does the decision help our company achieve our stated objectives? Are departments aligned from a content perspective? Are we putting regions or countries at risk with the decision?

Sometimes, compromises are made based on political reasons or higher management decisions. It's not ideal, but as long as the team understands and acknowledges the changes, they can discuss how to modify the course and move forward.

In Summary

One person alone can't scale content across regions. Once we agree on objectives for the team, we still need to bring the objectives and plans to life. It requires relevant stakeholders from headquarters and local teams working together. If you are in headquarters, make an effort to understand the geography's challenges and the local markets. If you are in a region or country, please speak up and voice your opinions and needs. Regions are headquarters' BFF in global marketing coordination. Create a win–win scenario by coming together, staying together, and working together.

> *If you are in headquarters, make an effort to understand the geography's challenges and the local markets.*

3A's for People: **Assemble** the right people to **Align** on the same goals and **Act** with a sense of trust and clearly defined roles.

3 C's for Process: **Collaborate** by agreeing on plans, processes, and tools. **Communicate** by setting up a regular schedule to discuss issues and resolutions. **Compromise** by making hard calls on priorities collectively.

If you're a headquarters representative, here are three tips to remember:

▶ Be a good listener. It's easy to fall into the mentality that you should tell people what to do. Change this mentality and remember your job is to support the geographies.

▶ Ask a lot of questions. Understand the local needs. You can then prioritize these needs and what you think is best to support them.

▶ You are here to serve.

A lasting relationship needs to start with headquarters. If the global content marketing manager demonstrates that he or she is determined to help and make the company and geographies successful, stakeholders will reciprocate. I firmly believe the statement from Napoleon Hill: "It is literally true that you can succeed best and quickest by helping others to succeed."[8] Cross-regional content planning is not hard to do as long as headquarters keeps locals' needs in mind. Headquarters should provide leadership and support while empowering geographies with the autonomy to do their jobs. Regions need to understand that headquarters' hands may be tied with product delays, politics, and departmental silos. A productive working relationship needs to be built over a period of time. Collaboration can't be achieved by one face-to-face meeting or ad hoc communications only. Like any other relationship, both sides need to put in time and effort. Now, it's time to dive into the 4 P's stages of global content marketing cycle. Let the fun begin.

> *It is literally true that you can succeed best and quickest by helping others to succeed.*

For Entrepreneurs and Small Businesses Owners

▶ If your company is small but you are moving quickly in several countries, provide high-level guidance and goals, and hire competent people to manage your local marketing efforts. If you can't afford to hire anyone yet, focus on sales instead of content marketing for the time being.

▶ Timely communication is essential to build solid relationships.

▶ It may make sense to decentralize and let geographies take the lead initially to drive growth without much limitation.

For Enterprise Marketing Managers

▶ Align business objectives and strategies. Determine geographies' priorities and needs.

▶ Schedule a regular time to meet and discuss issues.

▶ If either side needs to say no to specific requests, be prepared to back up the decision with reasons based on logic and data.

For Agencies and Marketing Consultants

▶ Help clients identify content challenges and needs.

▶ Share other clients' best practices.

▶ Proactively recommend processes and tools to address their issues.

Act with Headquarters as the Lead: Global Personas

Before we market our products, we must know to whom we market. In the world of global content marketing, agreeing up front on a set of audiences that we are targeting will ensure smooth upcoming content discussion and collaboration. Each geography may have different go-to-market plans and campaigns, but we must agree on objectives (what) and audience (who).

Personifying the audience with a name allows the team to start a conversation from the outset. It allows you to become familiar with your target audience and create content with a "face" in mind. Creating a persona to represent a target audience is a typical part of Web or user experience design. Web designers need to understand for whom the Web page is created. A good persona provides insight and direction for wording, images, content, tone, and design. A persona is also essential for content planning, especially global content planning.

Because it's a global effort, the persona needs to be global in nature. Is it possible to create a global persona? The answer is "Yes" for some companies depending on their industry (manufacturing, healthcare, skincare, banking, and so on) and products (homogenous or highly localized across regions). However, consumer-oriented products tend to be highly localized, due to local behavior and usage models. Therefore, localized personas make better sense than global personas. But some companies may require several personas to satisfy different geographies' needs based on audience segmentation.

At Intel, there are six global personas for consumer marketing and two for business marketing. When I spoke with Meagen Eisenberg, VP of Demand Gen at DocuSign,[9] she shared that there are twenty global personas for DocuSign, ranging from real estate agents to human resources managers. They target anyone who is over 18 and can send or sign documents.

The global persona creation needs to be led and owned by corporate with the regions and countries providing input. In a big enterprise, headquarters conducts qualitative and quantitative research across regions and countries. The trick is to find commonalities in your audiences across regions.

For example, a 20-year-old Millennial in Beijing may not listen to the same music as one who lives in Munich. However, their love of music and constant use of a headset are common threads; IT managers in Brazil and in Russia may have different network infrastructures, but they are equally concerned about security threats. Zoom in on common challenges, pain points, and needs and desires they share. In order to scale content cross regionally, it's important to have a global persona to rally headquarters and geographic teams so they are clear about the audiences they need to reach. If headquarters and countries can't agree on the target audience, it's almost impossible to move to the next level of planning and execution.

SMBs don't typically have the budget to create a formal global persona. That's OK! If no one in your marketing organization owns the persona creation or discussion, start one yourself by talking to your sales representatives and conducting your own phone interviews with customers in multiple countries. Create an informal slide or document with your findings. Here are some details to include:

- ▶ Demographics
- ▶ Behavioral Attributes
- ▶ Target Audience Budget Range
- ▶ Device Usages
- ▶ Communications Preferences
- ▶ Content Format Preferences
- ▶ Job Descriptions
- ▶ Recommended Keywords

Don't stress out! Again, you don't need all the criteria listed above. For global content planning, at a minimal level, it's important to know:

- ▶ Job Description
- ▶ Pain Points, Challenges, Needs and Desires
- ▶ Communications Preferences
- ▶ Content Format Preferences

Essentially, you need to know what your target audiences' challenges, needs, and desires are, and where they go to find content. Document the persona as much as you can and share that with key stakeholders. It's OK to create an informal persona and validate that with relevant stakeholders such as your sales, web marketing, or even your product team. This persona will serve as your basis for content.

A persona is a living document. The way your persona prefers and consumes content will change over time. At Intel, the persona is refreshed every two to three years.

Think about this: the way we consumed content before smartphones and the way content is consumed now are vastly different. Device usage and technology play important roles that should be reflected in your persona description. Ultimately, the insight will help your content planning and content creation, especially when it comes to content for mobile device consumption. You need to be cognizant of formats, images, font sizes, and length.

Please bear in mind that a persona is a compass, not a panacea:

- ▶ It's a tool to help you and your team understand your audience.
- ▶ It's a tool for editorial and content planning.
- ▶ It's a living document.
- ▶ A persona can be created formally or informally. Personal discovery and development can be driven top-down or bottom-up.

A good persona provides insights into your audiences' attitudes, purchasing behavior, thought process, challenges and desires. It gives you guidance on what content to create and where to syndicate it. Although we attempt to create a global persona by focusing on commonalities, let's not lose what makes the audience unique in local regions. This is where the regional marketing team needs to come forward to share its insights on localizing and translating of global content or global campaigns. ***A global persona does not equate to global content and a global media plan.*** Customization and localization of content is still necessary with localized social media and paid media plans.

Communication Through Sync Meetings: There Is No Shortage of Agenda Items

Coming up with agenda items or topics to discuss at the weekly sync meetings with regions and country teams is challenging. When I speak at conferences about setting up regular meetings between headquarters and regions, the audience often asks how to fill the time slot of regular sync meetings. There really isn't a shortage of agenda topics. The best way to build the agenda is to talk to your team members, both at headquarters and in the regions, to understand what they want to hear and discuss at the meetings. Here are some examples that my geographical counterparts find useful:

- ► Company's worldwide sales goals and business objectives (e.g., plan changes in the fast-paced environment) and updates
- ► Corporate-wide marketing plans and metrics
- ► Product roadmap (this can change often, too)
- ► Messaging, product positioning, content plans
- ► Creative and style playbook based on marketing campaign themes
- ► Branding guide for master and product brands/logos
- ► Primary and secondary marketing research and trends
- ► Country marketing plans, marketing metrics, sales results
- ► Country's challenges and needs
- ► Editorial and content discussion
- ► Budget discussion
- ► Lead generation
- ► Content localization and translation
- ► Sales discounts and offerings
- ► Co-marketing with partners and channel partners
- ► Third-party speaker or agency sharing new trends
- ► Sales and marketing collaboration

- ▶ Tools to track measurement
- ▶ New tools to pilot
- ▶ Best practices sharing between geographies
- ▶ Social media
- ▶ Innovation campaigns by different countries
- ▶ Paid media buy
- ▶ Web site design and updates

As a chairperson, you do not need to create a presentation for all the topics mentioned previously, but you need to find appropriate people within the company to come to the meetings to discuss the topics and share their insights. Not every topic needs a presentation; sometimes a roundtable or free-form discussion can also be very effective. As a participant, volunteer to present and contribute agenda topics. Once you start the meeting, you will be surprised by the number of other topics that pop-up. Always publish your agendas in advance, but if you have nothing to talk about, it's always appropriate to cancel the meetings and give the time back to everyone. No one will complain about that.

CHAPTER FOUR

The First P of the Global Content Marketing Cycle: Plan

Definition of Plan

Collaborate with relevant stakeholders on regional and country teams to create a global content marketing strategy that aligns target audiences, key success metrics, priority countries, and strategic editorial topics with your business objectives. Alignment of objectives and strategy is vital because it dictates content creation, promotion and measurement.

> *"Plan your work for today and everyday, then work on your plan"*
> **—MARGARET THATCHER**[1]

To Plan or Not to Plan

For most of us, planning is in our DNA. We plan our weddings, our vacations, even our days—sometimes to increments of less than an hour. Even if you are not a planner yourself, your days are somehow organized or scheduled for you by someone else; an "invisible hand." There are inherent benefits to planning that we all recognize:

- ▶ Have an active path to accomplish end goals
- ▶ Mitigate foreseeable chaos

Through the plan, the future you will see. . . . OK, I sound like Yoda.

So, plan it is! But here is the irony of planning that frustrates us: we spend so much time and effort planning, yet things usually do not work out the way we plan. Chaos intervenes—perhaps the budget is reduced due to changes in the business environment, or the product is delayed. Maybe we should just . . . *do* things instead.

Planning is an active way of discussing the goals, objectives, strategies, and tasks that we need to accomplish. Plans are the documentation of planning.

The truth is there is a difference between "plans" and "planning." Planning is an active way of discussing the goals, objectives, strategies, and tasks that we need to accomplish. Plans are the documentation of planning. Because things change, plans need to be updated on a regular basis. Planning is a continuous process that helps us adjust course, keep on track, and make accomplishing our goals more likely.

President Eisenhower said it so poignantly: "In preparing for battle I have always found that plans are useless, but planning is indispensable."[2] ***Planning is the prerequisite of business success, but success is not guaranteed by planning.***

Here are three key differences between planning and plans:

- ▶ Planning is an active ongoing process, while plans are the documentation of that discussion at one point in time.
- ▶ Planning aims to mitigate problems and changes, yet bears in mind that the only constant in life is change. Your plan will change as you go.
- ▶ Neither planning nor a plan guarantees success, yet both are absolutely essential.

These following two quotes reflect perspectives on the planning process. Jennifer Baichwal, a documentary filmmaker, expresses a critical point: "Have a plan, but be ready to abandon it at any moment."[3] Of course, Yogi Berra's Yogi-isms are always enlightening: "If you don't know where you are going, you'll end up someplace else."[4]

So don't fall in love with your marketing plans. Don't get frustrated with constant changes. It's all part of the game and that is especially true in a fast-paced, changing environment.

A Plan is a documentation to prepare for replanning. The saga of planning never ends.

> *A Plan is a documentation to prepare for replanning. The saga of planning never ends.*

A Plan Before the Global Content Plan: The Granddaddy of All Marketing Plans

There is a pre-step before starting your global content plan. It's a 20,000 foot view of your company's overall marketing landscape. Ultimately, the Granddaddy of all marketing plans gives you ammunition to complete your global content plan. Essentially, it's the prework you need to do to ensure the global content plan is comprehensive and aligned with your company's objectives and needs. You may ask yourself, is this the responsibility of content marketing? Ideally, no. But if this strategic plan doesn't exist you need to work with management to have it created.

In general, *marketing plan* is a generic term. You will notice that each marketing function creates its own marketing plan. If you work in the events department, you create an event marketing plan. If you work on direct marketing, you create a direct marketing plan. If you are a community and social media manager, you create a social media marketing plan. However, events, social media, and direct marketing are merely channels of your company's marketing engine. There has to be a big overall plan before each marketing department can create its own plan that will be effective as part of a coordinated whole.

> *A plan's preplan provides key strategic elements to ensure everyone will achieve the same business objectives.*

Scaling content globally does not happen accidentally or spontaneously. It requires careful planning. You have to stage it. Before each marketing department can create its own version of a marketing plan and before you can create your global content plan, a higher-level strategic direction needs to be created. Think of it as a plan's preplan, which provides some key strategic elements to ensure everyone across all regions will move in the same direction and work toward achieving the same business objectives. Think of this high-level marketing plan as the Granddaddy of all marketing plans.

This Granddaddy of all marketing plans tends to be ignored or overlooked by many of us because we really don't need it to do our day-to-day jobs. If your job is to get 5,000 leads a month, do you need the Granddaddy of all marketing plans? You know your job, you know your goal, and you just . . . do it!

Here lies the predicament: For the 5,000 leads per month that you need to generate across three countries, you may buy a list from one country, gather the leads from trade shows and industry events in another country, or receive leads from local sales reps in a third country. To know what to do, you need to talk to your local teams and do some research. Do leads from each country have the same value and potential for achieving the overall corporate goals? You also need to know the targeted industry segments and target audiences, business goals and a list of priority countries. You need to find these answers within the Granddaddy of all marketing plans.

Perhaps another option to generate 5,000 leads a month is to run regular e-mail campaigns to nurture those leads in three countries. In order to run your regular e-mail campaigns, you need information that is relevant and helpful to your customers. Again, topical content planning and product messaging should be heavily informed by the audience segmentation in the Granddaddy of all marketing plans.

This master marketing plan will help you connect some dots before creating your global content strategy map. It guides us so our subsidiary marketing plans align with the company's overall business directions and targets the appropriate audience. According to *The 4 Disciplines of Execution* by Chris McChesney, Sean Covey, and Jim Huling, "Only 15% of employees actually know their organization's most important goals—either there are no goals or they have too many goals . . . ." Before having a conversation with management, the first step is to align your global content plan with the business objectives and goals. Understand what's important to the company and position the value of content in a way that management can understand (see Figure 4.01).

PLAN

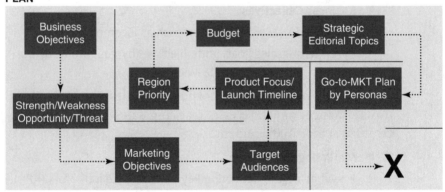

FIGURE 4.01 "The Essential Elements of Global Content Plan"

The benefits of the Granddaddy of all marketing plans:

▶ Align global content plans and strategy with business and marketing objectives.

▶ Identify agreed-upon target audiences with relevant stakeholders before editorial planning.

▶ Incorporate key growth countries as part of the global content plan.

> *In order to connect the dots, you need to know where and what the dots are. The Granddaddy of all marketing plans reveals core relevant dots.*

▶ Gauge the projected budget's adequacy for content needs.

▶ Recognize potential content gaps to drive discussions with relevant stakeholders.

In order to connect the dots, you need to know where and what the dots are. The Granddaddy of all marketing plans reveals core relevant dots.

So, what does the Granddaddy of all marketing plans entail?

Key Elements for the Granddaddy of All Marketing Plans

In general, here are key elements to include:

▶ **Business Objectives**:

   ▶ What do we want to accomplish as a company?

   ▶ What are sales goals and objectives by geography, by business unit, and corporate-wide?

Possible Sources: CEO's office, the sales teams, business units, finance, or whoever is tracking sales goals and objectives for senior management.

▶ **Marketing Objectives:**

   ▶ What are the marketing key performance indicators (KPIs) you will target and track?

   ▶ How can you link your marketing objectives to the business objectives? (KPIs may need to be stated in such a way that they address a business objective, for example, increase market share for new product line by 15 percent.)

Possible Sources: CEO's office, CMO's office, marketing strategy teams.

▶ **Competitive Landscape**:

   ▶ What do the industry and product trends look like by region or key countries?

   ▶ What are competitors doing? Are there any local or regional competitors that we need to be aware of?

- ► How do our products compare to our competitors? How do we differentiate?
- ► Are there newcomers that we need to be aware of?

Possible Sources: Business units, sales, product teams, online search, primary marketing research and third-party research, regional and country sales and marketing teams.

- ► **Customers and Audiences**:
  - ► What is the makeup of our customers and audiences?
  - ► Are our customers the same across regions? If not, how should we serve different sets of customers and audiences?

Possible Sources: Marketing, business units, product team or sales, marketing research.

- ► **Product and/or Service Focus**:
  - ► What is the priority list of products and/or services we should market?
  - ► Will that differ from region to region? If yes, how would that impact global content strategy?
  - ► Where in the product life cycle do our products fall?
  - ► What are different services we offer to different markets?

Possible Sources: Marketing, business units, and sales. Regional and local sales and marketing teams.

- ► **Priority Countries and/or Regions**:
  - ► Where are potential or desirable growth areas or growth segments?
  - ► Where will our key focus be?
  - ► What is the support structure from corporate and at the local level?

Possible Sources: Marketing, sales, business units, finance, regional and/or country sales and marketing teams.

- ► **Product Positioning and Messaging**:
  - ► Why should our audience care?
  - ► Why do they need to buy from us?
  - ► When they buy from us, what are they really buying?
  - ► What are their pain points, challenges, and aspirations?

Possible Sources: Marketing, business units, product groups, marketing research.

► **Budget**:
- ► What is the proposed marketing budget and allocation by business unit and by geography?
- ► Is the budget centralized or decentralized?
- ► What is the company's budget allocation process?

Possible Sources: Marketing, finance, business units, or sales (depending on budget structure in your company).

As you can see, possible sources of information really depend on the organizational structure, corporate culture, and roles and responsibilities of divisional functions. ***The information is scattered around, and you may need to do a scavenger hunt***. Ask around, starting with your manager and your own group first. Most of the information you need lies within finance, sales, business units and/or product groups, research, marketing, and regional and/or country offices. If you search diligently and you can't find information you require, make assumptions based on prior experience and move forward.

Business objective is to sell 100 software systems, but marketing objective establishes our system superiority over competition.

Understanding business objectives and sales goals is easy; but we need to think through how to translate that to marketing objectives. A business objective may be to sell 100 software systems in the healthcare segment, but the marketing objective can be to establish our systems as a preferred choice for healthcare IT managers. Some marketing objectives may not directly tie to sales and leads, but spending time up front to determine suitable marketing objectives helps guide your marketing activities and content planning.

Any time and effort you put into understanding your company's overall direction, business goals, product priorities, growth areas, and audience won't be wasted, and you may even feel that a lot of information is missing when you move on to creating your content.

At the stage of gathering intelligence, you can also gauge how your company views content. Is it an afterthought? Is it a front and center priority for your marketing organization? Do they care? Do they even know what content means? Do they know what content does? Understanding the culture will help you determine how you want to manage content communications and plan accordingly.

Finally, Let's Get the Party Started: Global Content Planning

Now you have a basic understanding of business objectives, customers, product and country priorities, and the budget process. It's time to create the global content plan! So, what should be included in the global content plan?

Key Elements of a Global Content Plan

The purpose of a global content plan is to align headquarters, regions and countries, content creators, the Web team, the media team, and other marketing departments that create, publish, and curate content. On a strategic level it is essential to identify editorial topics and product launch timelines before content creation and execution. You also need to understand where your audience goes to find content so that you can determine the suitable formats for placement and syndication.

It's important to have someone at headquarters take the lead in coordinating with the relevant stakeholders to create a global content plan. Ideally, if there will be a content strategist or an editor-in-chief for the company, this person will naturally take the lead in creating the global content plan. If not, someone needs to take the lead to coordinate with the stakeholders. This person can be a campaign manager, a content creator, a web marketing manager, a brand manager, or someone who is passionate about content.

The benefits of a global content plan:

▶ Aligns relevant stakeholders who work on content

> ▶ Justifies the budget you need
> ▶ Shows management you know what you are doing

Here are the key elements of a global content plan:
Information from your Granddaddy of all marketing plans:

> ▶ Business objectives and company goals
> ▶ Marketing objectives
> ▶ Growth segments and countries
> ▶ Target customers
> ▶ Product focus and launches

Additional information to add to the global content plan:

> ▶ High-level editorial calendar, including content topics, key product launches, key seasonal sales periods, and major corporate and PR events
> ▶ Target customers by personas
> ▶ Go-to-market (GTM) plan for each persona

A global content plan should be succinct and limited to no more than 10–15 PowerPoint slides or a 3–5 page brief. Choose a format that is easy for you to share with your team. It should be at a strategic level and provide the information necessary to guide stakeholders who will use it as a baseline for the next level of detailed content planning for content production.

Here are examples of each element for your consideration. You can certainly modify the statements to fit your needs.

Business and Marketing Objectives

Sales objective examples:

> ▶ Increase sales from $10 million to $15 million in the healthcare segment.
> ▶ Increase profit margin from 7 percent to 10 percent.
> ▶ Grow the new financial services segment from $0 to $5 million in China.

Brand objective examples:

▶ Increase brand recognition from 15 percent to 17 percent after two product launches in the United States, the United Kingdom, Germany, and France.

▶ Increase brand relevance from 30 percent to 35 percent with premier certified channel partners.

Customer service objective examples:

▶ Improve customer service by launching web chat and responding to e-mail requests within 24 hours.

▶ Decrease customer response time by 15 percent from baseline.

Most companies measure their success by revenue, market share, and profit. Some companies also focus on brand awareness or brand equity. You need to understand how your company measures success. If your company has not formally defined goals, work with your sales team to understand their quotas. If your company has too many goals, you need to narrow them down to two or three goals that you will be able to support. ***Be very focused.*** You likely won't have enough budget and resources to support too many initiatives, so determine which goals are supported by your global content plan and get buy-in from management. Be prepared to answer why you selected these goals over others. Crisp business and marketing objectives will inform your direction for content planning.

> *If your company has too many goals, you need to narrow them down to two or three goals that you will be able to support. Be very focused.*

Key growth segment and country priority examples:

▶ Open 40 sandwich and coffee shops in the United Kingdom and Canada by recruiting 15 franchise partners.

▶ Grow solar panel sales for residential and commercial properties in the United States and Australia.

Some companies will have a roadmap for the countries and segments in which they want to grow. Again, this tends to be directed by corporate, not regions. If your company wants to grow internationally, you need to understand where they want to go and in what segment they would like to expand. It will help you determine requirements related to language and localization of content.

If your company doesn't have a plan to expand to other regions, but you notice people from other regions are consuming your content, you should explore why they consume your content and understand if there is any purchase intent. You never know—you may be able to turn them into customers.

Key Success Metrics (Marketing Specific)

Inbound metrics examples:

▶ Drive 10 percent growth month over month in organic (i.e., not paid) web traffic from the United States, Australia, and the United Kingdom for leads and opportunities through targeted content marketing.

▶ Grow leads from inbound traffic by 30 percent.

Outbound metrics examples:

▶ Drive social engagements with potential customers by syndicating five content pieces to target social channels five days a week.

▶ Aid the customer service department by responding to customers' questions through Twitter and Facebook within three hours. Share content to answer questions as appropriate.

Tie Global Content Plan Elements to Business Objectives and Metrics

Content can only play a critical role as part of the marketing strategy if content is quantified as part of the success metrics that management cares about.

If one of the key objectives of a global content plan is to get all relevant stakeholders aligned, then the success metrics need to tie content to business objectives. Content can only play a critical role as part of the marketing strategy if content is quantified as part of the success metrics that management cares about. As part of the global content plan, you need to identify what the metrics are that determine success. If it's about sales, then your content metrics need to contribute to leads and potential sales opportunities. If it's about brand awareness and equity, your content metrics need to tie to overall marketing campaigns that drive brand awareness. If it's about customer service, is it possible to identify certain formats of customer service training to accelerate customer response time? Setting up key metrics can be time-consuming, but it's worth the time if the metrics are meaningful enough to focus marketing efforts to drive management goals. There are different types of success metrics that management will find valuable, if you position them in the right way. I will discuss metrics more in Chapter 7.

Target Customers by Personas

Personas are archetypal characters created to represent the different user types within a targeted demographic, attitude, or behavior set that might use a site, brand, or product a similar way.[5] They are a representation of the goals and behaviors of a hypothesized group of potential and ideal customers that you would like to reach. A good persona provides insight and direction for wording/copy, images, content, tone, and design. A persona is also essential for content planning, especially global content planning. Personas inform you what content to create and where content should be syndicated. Refer to the Global Persona Case Study in Chapter 3.

Editorial Calendar and Product Launches

Editorial topics you select should address audiences' challenges, pain points, needs, and desires. Make the topics broad enough so that it's easy for you to improvise and create various specific editorial topics. For example, healthy living is a broad topic. You can discuss the subcategory topics such as food, fitness, alcohol, mental health, stress management,

> *It's important to pick a topic to address your audiences' needs directly or indirectly.*

and more. It's important to pick a topic to address your audience's needs directly or indirectly. Editorial topics are a means to build relevance and a relationship or conversations with your audience. Inject your products and services, where and when it's appropriate.

The best way to showcase the strategic value of content to senior management is through an annual strategic editorial calendar. ***Management loves to see that you have a plan; you know what to do and when you're going to do it***. It gives them a sense of confidence. Even if you don't have a completed calendar, use one page to succinctly show the key editorial topics and product launches to management in the interim.

Create a Go-to-Market Plan for Each Persona

It's important to show the marketing channels you will use to engage with your target customers. For some audiences, you will only target print and e-mail. For other audiences, social media is absolutely essential. As part of the global content plan, it's useful to share go-to-market channels, even though it's only directional guidance that is subject to change. The information will be helpful to guide the subsequent stages of content production and promotion.

How to Position Content to Management

"After all is said and done, more is said than done." —Aesop. In most companies, content is an afterthought in both sales and marketing groups. We talk about marketing in the context of advertising, campaign creative concepts, events, training, Web sites, user experiences, in-store designs, and social media. Content tends not to be part of any marketing functions' plans. Here are a couple of recommendations to bring content to the table and get some love:

- ▶ Explain how content can help your internal customers
- ▶ Quantify content's impact

Explain How Content Can Help Your Internal Customers

When in Rome, do as the Romans do. Take your global content plan to various marketing divisions. Explain what the global content plan is and how the respective marketing groups can benefit. If you talk to events marketing, explain or show the type of content you will create and how that content can be part of booths, demos, and training sessions. If you talk to the Web marketing team, ask for their participation and involvement in determining the appropriate formats of content. Volunteer to help them on the offer and lead generation pages. Explain the benefits of the global content plan in a way the other marketing functions can understand and use to derive benefit. Let them know that you are here to *help* them.

Quantify Content's Impact

If content is something that no one is familiar with, including senior management, why don't you use the global content plan to position yourself as a thought leader? Explain to senior management how the content aligns with business and marketing objectives, illustrate how content is woven into various marketing functions, and how you will measure the impact which I will address more in Chapter 7. Management may be skeptical, but they are likely to listen and give you a chance if you are well prepared. This will be a continuous education process. Regular updates to management are absolutely essential to ensure that content is in their minds. Again, you need to tie content marketing efforts to business goals.

You may not know which exact approach will work at your company. You need to give it a try and adjust as necessary.

- ▶ Educate your senior managers.
- ▶ Align with other marketing departments and sales groups.
- ▶ Find content alliances in business units, finance, or any place with a passion for content.

Here is a reality check . . .

- ▶ It's OK to not know everything.
- ▶ It's important to get relevant stakeholders aligned on objectives and metrics.
- ▶ Global means targeting regions with intention.

> *We make decisions based on the limited data we have at a specific point in time. It's called informed risk taking. Make assumptions and move on.*

While gathering answers for the master marketing plan or the global content plan, a lot of questions will come up. You will have answers for some and others will require more research. We make decisions based on the limited data we have at a specific point in time. It's called informed risk taking. Make assumptions and move on.

I strongly believe that once all your stakeholders agree on what you want to accomplish as a team and how to measure success, everything else will follow. Make an effort to get everyone aligned.

Creating a global content plan is not a spontaneous or random action. Even with global personas, you still need to target specific regions or countries. If your company does not have specific countries in mind, I'd recommend that you look at your Web site reports and determine the countries with audiences that consistently come to your site. Find out why they visit and explore to see if there is any opportunity to serve them.

In Summary

Focus on the global content plan at a *strategic* level. Most of us would like to dive into the "tactics" immediately, addressing such concerns as what content to create and what formats to produce. Don't do that just yet. Sit back and think what you would like to accomplish first and how content can help your company.

One of the key purposes of your global content plan is to rally relevant internal stakeholders and geographies. Use the global content plan as a contract to get the relevant team members in agreement before moving to execution.

Planning is not hard, and what I am sharing is common sense. As Stephen Covey said in his bestseller *The 7 Habits of Highly Effective People*, **"Common sense isn't always common practice."**[6] Common practice means taking time to gather intelligence and find the seemingly unrelated dots to connect. It's pretty hard to quantify the Return on Investment (ROI) of planning, yet it's completely essential. One thing is for sure: if you want to be strategic about content on a global scale, plan ahead and be ready to modify your plan as needed. Being flexible and adaptable does not mean spontaneous or random. However, there is a "serendipity" element that I will address in Chapter 7.

Here is another secret of any global plan: your planning needs to be done in collaboration with geographic counterparts to ensure local feedback is taken into consideration. A global content plan is a shared effort between headquarters and the regions to define a high-level editorial roadmap with content recommendations to reach the target audience across marketing channels. Now that you have a global content plan, let's move to the second "P" for the global marketing cycle: Produce.

For Entrepreneurs and Small Businesses Owners

▶ If you don't have a big marketing budget, the best way to market yourself is through your knowledge and expertise. Focus on how your expertise and knowledge can solve your audience's pain points, challenges, and needs.

▶ Any new business can be chaotic. You are in the trenches slogging things out day-to-day. It's incredibly important to allocate time to plan. You can only grow if you plan ahead.

▶ It's OK to start small. Whether you start with a blog, videos, or some other format, implement something and keep a regular editorial calendar. There is no shortcut, hustle!

For Enterprise Marketing Managers

▶ Do your homework to gather the necessary information from preplan's plan to create your global content plan.

▶ Be flexible and adaptable, not random and spontaneous.

▶ It does take time, but it's worth it: Get all relevant stakeholders aligned with your objectives and metrics, if at all possible.

For Agencies and Marketing Consultants

▶ Encourage your clients to create a global content plan with the core elements listed in this chapter.

▶ A lot of the information gathering needs to be done by the clients. Guide them from the sidelines and make an effort to have a holistic view of your client's needs. Most of the time, clients write a brief to update you. Can you write a brief to your clients to show you understand their business?

▶ You may have plan-related information already. Help your client package it up.

CASE STUDY

Enterprise: Intel's Annual Planning Process

Intel's annual planning process is called "Plan [year]." The planning process for 2015 is called Plan 2015. This is a formal process that's both global and corporate-wide in nature. It is both a top-down and a bottom-up approach. Each division within a group will create its own plans. Divisional plans will roll up as part of the group plan. Each geographical region will also roll up its plan to headquarters. During the planning process, a lot of face-to-face meetings will occur within divisions and groups and geographies to ensure two-way discussions. Finance members in each department will also roll up each group's proposed budget requests as part of the plan. Finance, marketing research and business units will also gather competitive information, industry data, audience insights, and even macro and micro economic trends.

The process usually kicks off in September and lasts until the end of the year. Ultimately, each group will present its plan to the CEO in November. The CEO will review and finalize the corporate-wide plan, after which the company's business directions, sales goals for each group, and budget will be distributed in the December time frame. Given that Intel is a global company, Plan [year] strategic imperatives and goals will be communicated through multiple forums worldwide throughout the first quarter of the year. This planning period may seem chaotic and fluid, yet everyone seems to know what needs to be done and how to do it, partially because the timeline is clearly communicated to the employees who are responsible for the plans. Intel has displayed the discipline to do this year after year.

Here is where the corporate marketing group takes the lead and the regions and countries follow. In order to pave the way for regional and country marketing teams to start their Annual Plan, the headquarters' marketing team needs to work with product groups and marketing research to understand the product roadmap, industry and product competitive landscape, volume forecast and audience profiles four to six weeks prior to the official kick-off of the Annual Planning Cycle. A annual global marketing Plan needs to be created so that regional and country marketing can use it to create their detailed plans. At Intel, this global plan also includes some elements of a global content plan for business marketing. Specific elements such as audience needs and pain points, annual and quarterly editorial topics, and high-level deliverable timelines are incorporated into this master marketing plan.

Geographies use this master plan to ensure the plans they create are aligned with strategy. If some geographies need to deviate from the marketing strategy, the headquarters and geographies have a very frank discussion to determine the right solution to move forward. The 3 C's of working together as a team, communication, collaboration, and compromise, are keys in the annual planning process.

CASE STUDY

Small Business: Opus Events Agency's Planning Process

Opus Events Agency is an 85-person[7] event agency located in Portland, Oregon. You may not have heard of them, but you have very likely attended some of the events they produced without knowing it. They are the invisible hand that pulls together well-known large-scale or private events for many major enterprises. This company has been growing over 20 percent annually for the past eight years,[8] even through the deep recession of 2008.[9] Monte Wood, the president of the company, attributes the growth to thorough planning and highly competent people. In talking to Monte, I was amazed at how disciplined this company is in setting a long-term vision and short-term objectives and goals.

Monte points out that planning never really stops at Opus Events Agency. A formal process and timeline are in place. Select employees in each department are directly involved in the planning process, in addition to senior managers. The planning follows both a top-down and bottom-up approach. The company focuses its planning on both strategic and operational levels. With the new fiscal year starting on January 1, the strategic plan kicks off in March (Wow!), during which each department will conduct its own SWOT (Strengths, Weaknesses, Opportunities, and Threats) analysis by gathering industry competitive information. The reason to start in March is to give direction and allow each group to gather necessary information for the upcoming planning reviews. Senior staff will meet in June to review departmental SWOTs, competitive analysis, and other internal and external data to discuss the potential strategic directions for the next year.

There are several agenda-driven planning sessions between June and October to finalize both strategic and operational plans. By November, senior staff allocates budgets for each department based on the annual goals.

By January, senior staff hosts a one-day company-wide off-site meeting at which the company's direction and strategy for the upcoming year is openly shared and clearly communicated. This planning cycle ends with a big party for all employees to conclude the off-site meeting. Senior management is very transparent about the company's performance, even though it's a privately held company. A quarterly update is held to share the good, the bad, and the ugly for that quarter. Every employee knows how the company is doing.

Opus Events Agency relies on this master planning to help grow its business. The company fully understands the value of planning and is committed to a disciplined process. The outcome of planning allows employees and management to come together as individuals and work together as a team to define and achieve common goals. I don't usually see this level of dedication from management of a small business in creating its annual plan. Although this company does not do content marketing, I thought its planning methodology was worth a mention in this "Plan" chapter. As Monte graciously points out: "Growth is nurtured through planning."

Often, we are all heads down and trying hard to get day-to-day tasks completed. Not every company needs to coordinate their planning nine months in advance. However, it's important to set time aside several months before your new fiscal year to determine the objectives and goals. Once you articulate your target destinations, each team can map their course, coordinate logistics, and prepare tools and accessories to reach the goals.

Four Annual Planning Quadrants

The plan stage is the most time-consuming and important stage of a global content marketing effort. Planning can be completed formally or informally. *It can also be done by top-down or bottom-up within an organization.* Understanding how your company's planning is done will expedite the effort of gathering the relevant information for your global content plan. If you know the planning approach of your company, you can easily weave and dodge when your plan changes.

Formal and Top-down: A company is small in size (not necessarily in revenue) with a small senior staff. The planning process, which determines corporate direction, usually starts a couple months before the new fiscal year and is led by the owner or senior executives of the company. Many of the core elements of the Granddaddy of all marketing plans will be discussed or shared in presentations during the planning meetings. Then, the CEO and senior staff will kick off the new fiscal year with a formal forum in which they communicate the plans and objectives to employees. If you need additional information for your marketing plans, you should be able to get it by talking to senior staff.

Formal, Top-down and Bottom-up: This is a typical process in big enterprises or multi-national companies (MNCs). A formal planning process will be kicked off one or two quarters before the new fiscal year. The planning may be a corporate-wide effort in which Senior VPs ask their divisions and their direct staff to roll up the budget and projects so that they can be presented to the CEO. At the same time, the CEO and senior management will have discussions of their own on strategy and the future direction of the company. This planning effort is a two-way street.

The bottoms-up plan will be consolidated by each division and presented to the CEO. The CEO, senior VPs, and Finance will use that and their own judgment to determine the key imperatives and allocate budget for the upcoming year. Then, the company direction and strategy will be rolled out through a series of formal communications such as webcasts, employee forums and internal conferences. In this case, all the core elements of the master marketing plan are in formal presentations and documents. You may need to sift through lengthy presentations to pull the relevant information you need but the data for your global content planning should be available.

Informal and Top-down: This tends to happen in smaller companies where the CEO or owners are in charge. The planning process is usually informal, so you likely need to interview your CEO and a couple of other senior managers to get information for your global content planning. Document your discoveries and validate the information with them.

Informal, Top-down and Bottoms-up: This is a little messy, since there is no formal planning process to get everyone aligned. Again, it's more likely to happen in smaller companies. Focus on working with key senior managers and be prepared to gather a lot of information and do a lot of homework yourself. Again, it's important to document your discoveries and validate the information with the management team.

The best timing to create global content plan is during your company's annual planning process. Each company's planning process and timing is different. Volunteering to be part of the planning process will help you tremendously understand who's who and how marketing is done within your company.

CHAPTER FIVE

The Second P of the Global Content Marketing Cycle: Produce

Develop relevant stories that meet identified countries' needs with different formats based on strategic editorial topics that address the target audience's pain points, desires, and challenges. Use tools and data to optimize continuous content production.

> *"The creation of a thousand forests is in one acorn."*
>
> **—RALPH WALDO EMERSON**

We All Struggle to Create the Content We Need

The Plan chapter discussed how to create a strategic global content marketing plan that ties with a company's business and marketing objectives. It emphasizes that content planning

With or without a global content plan or regular sync meetings, content has been generated within the organization.

should be part of the corporate-wide planning process. As a result, a holistic content plan is created to rally the headquarters and local teams. Sounds great, right?

Here is the reality: with or without a global content plan or regular sync meetings, content has been generated within the organization, regardless of the size of a company. Somehow, blogs have been written, Facebook pages have been updated, sales collateral has been created, and product information has been uploaded to Web sites. The timing may be off, the frequency may be scarce, the format may not be ideal, and the quality of content may not be the best, but one way or another, content was created. This does not mean that content is created for the sake of creation itself. According to people who create or manage the content, they all serve some sort of purpose. But content creators may not understand how their content fits into the overall corporate picture or even if others in the company are creating similar content. They may not understand the full value of their content or realize that it can be repurposed for other forms of communications. For example, the one-page collateral created for the sales team to share with their customers may be reused for events as a flyer. Yet no one evaluates the content to help the content creator or the sales team connect that dot. Most of us do not think about the multiuse potential of content as we create it for a specific tactical purpose. To maximize the value of our content production efforts, it's important to understand what your company already has and find ways to leverage that content.

In informal conversations with my industry peers, it has become clear to me that there is no standard process to produce content. Every company, and even different divisions within the same company, has its own process or lack thereof. The different content creation processes in each company reminds me of how everyone takes different creative approaches to writing. Some people go for a walk; some people listen to loud music. Everyone's creative process is a little different, yet something wonderful comes out of it. That's also how it works for the company's content creation process. Regardless of the size of a company, there is always a struggle to create the required content.

This struggling usually comes from:

- ▶ Lack of clear leadership for content production: a lot of people create content, but no one really leads and owns the process.
- ▶ Lack of a current inventory list: understanding the past informs the future. Someone should have a clear understanding of the current content inventory related to key products or strategic editorial topics that can help guide future content planning.
- ▶ Lack of holistic content production program management: people create content because a request comes from someone to serve one specific communication purpose. However, the content creator or content requestor does not know how this piece of content fits into the overall company's content landscape and upcoming content pipeline.
- ▶ Lack of regular sync meetings to keep content producers in the loop: there is no forum to keep content creators informed.
- ▶ Lack of clear product and topical oriented messaging and/or story framework: content creators need high-level guidance on what to say and how to say it for specific products and topics.

You Have the Power to Make a Difference

If you are overwhelmed by reading the "lack of" list, take a deep breath. No matter the size of a company or management commitment, we can always start with a baby step. No, we can't change the organizational structure. No, we likely can't stop any content creation in process. No, we may not even know who is creating what. However, depending on our roles, we can always do little things to help others:

- ▶ Start by reaching out to others who are doing a similar job and understand what they are creating.
- ▶ Pull several content creators together on a biweekly basis just to informally talk about what content has been created and what is planned.

► Compare notes on messaging and story framework with other content creators.

► Invite webmaster or digital marketers to informal gatherings in which we tell them what we create and see if they can use it.

► Create our own content pipeline list.

► Reach out to a few countries and understand what content they have created. Can they use the content we create?

► Find out our business and marketing objectives and determine if content we create ties to corporate objectives.

> *Make an effort to connect dots to enable grassroots momentum to create and share useful content.*

What are little steps you can take to connect more dots within divisions and within other regions? If anyone is making an effort to connect more dots, a grassroots effort can gain momentum and the creation of more useful content and sharing content with more channels will start. Sometimes the best way to start a movement is bottom-up. Through several people working together, a process starts to form. With more people joining, an informal process becomes formalized. I share a case study at the end of this chapter about a marketing manager who took baby steps with the little budget she has to create content. Although it's not global content marketing collaboration, it's inspiring to know how creative she is with just $1,000 per month.

When I posted a blog about taking baby steps to manage content, Christian De Neef commented: "Many content management efforts start with enthusiasm but are rapidly abandoned. Grassroots may be a good start, but in my experience both a little discipline and a supporting technology facilitating content management are needed to achieve something." De Neef is right that a bottom-up approach is hard to sustain in the long run. At some points, the bottom-up needs to be intersected by a top-down commitment in order to persevere in an organization. The clear signal that a grassroots effort is gaining momentum is when the organization or senior management assigns an editor, a content strategist or a content lead.

Global Content Production Requires Leadership and Management Commitment

Let's say the bottom-up process is gaining momentum and more people get involved, it's important to have an identified "leader." This is especially critical in global content production collaboration: *a content marketing lead is required*. This person may not have the "content marketing" manager title, but his or her roles and responsibilities need to include content marketing efforts. It's best if this person is from headquarters. While this does not mean that this person needs to be physically located at the headquarters' building, this leader should have corporate-wide responsibilities.

In small- and medium-sized businesses (SMBs), the content marketing lead has both corporate-wide and local responsibilities. Albert Jan (AJ) Huisman, Director Marketing & Business Development at Kennedy Van der Laan, one of the Netherlands top independent law firms[i] set up two marketing objectives after joining the firm in 2011:

- ▶ Establish the law firm's thought leadership in five sectors: Finance/Insurance, Technology, Healthcare, Media and Government.
- ▶ Grow additional revenue by creating new businesses and leads.

Even though he believes in content marketing, his management was skeptical and he started his content initiative with baby steps. Through continuous education and communication with his management, he was able to convince his partners to blog, create videos and speak at events about their areas of expertise. With a regular editorial calendar, he was able to build a wealth of content in various formats. Many of his best subject matter experts turned out to be his management team. Starting in 2013, he revamped their Web site and set up a marketing automation tool to track leads with e-mail campaigns. His team wears both the corporate and local hats.

Because the firm has close relations with other law firms in Europe and the United States, select content is translated to German, English, French and other languages. To echo Christian's comments, AJ also pointed out that leadership and management support are essential to sustain content marketing efforts in a long run.

> *Most content production initiatives start in an organic way with the headquarters and local in parallel.*

In a major enterprise, most content production initiatives start in an organic way with the headquarters and local in parallel. Here's one possible scenario for how to get things started: the corporate office starts creating product-related content to educate customers. Product-related content becomes useful features and tips content for our customers, and evolves to add how-to guides, product comparisons, or even predictions and trends to showcase the company's expertise. Different content is then created to educate customers at different stages of the purchase cycle and to facilitate the sales process.

Another scenario is that content is generated to create demand or nurture leads through direct marketing or e-mail campaigns. One other possible scenario is that someone in the corporate office simply starts blogging or creates a user community to allow users to congregate. To keep a community alive, fresh and timely content is necessary to entice community members to visit regularly.

Because headquarters has produced content already, for the sake of efficiency it makes sense to leverage the content for other regions. In reality, not all content translates or localizes well to other languages. When scaling from single country content production to global content production it is important to utilize your team at the local level and incorporate their input up front. In general, that's the best way to do it, but the collaboration process can be lengthy and content creation becomes a committee or consensus approach, which may impact the quality of results. Sometimes, you may need to reject certain local requests in order to maintain the content quality. Or the local team may reject corporate assets and completely create their own content. In addition, not all countries' content is created equally. If your company plans to penetrate specific countries, you need to weigh that in as part of the content creation process, which should be addressed in the global content planning process.

I have noticed that headquarters' teams from many companies continue to create content without much interaction with their local teams—they just share the finished content with them. This may work if the local teams have the resources and skills to then take the content list and determine which content to localize and translate. This model also works when the products are highly localized and the local team generates quite a lot of original content themselves. But this may not be very efficient. There is always a trade-off between cost and efficiency. As you can see, the global content production process varies from company to company and industry to industry.

Steps for Global Content Production

Once a leader is identified and a team of relevant players is assembled, you can start implementing a global content production plan. Below are recommended steps that most companies follow, although you can certainly modify the steps to tailor to your team's needs. The local team's feedback should be incorporated into each step, if possible (see Figure 5.01).

- ▶ Step 1: Agree on the target personas.
- ▶ Step 2: Have a sense of any existing content, either by topic or audience persona.
- ▶ Step 3: Brainstorm a list of relevant topics to discuss.
- ▶ Step 4: Map topics to an editorial calendar.
- ▶ Step 5: Identify owners to create content.
- ▶ Step 6: Manage and review content creation.
- ▶ Step 7: Publish the content for others to access.
- ▶ Step 8: Create a content kit to share with the local teams.

PRODUCE

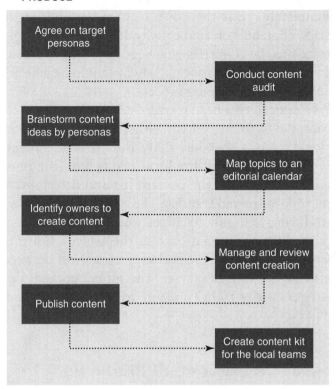

FIGURE 5.01 Steps to Produce Global Content

Step 1: Produce Content with a Purpose and a Persona in Mind

No matter how different everyone's content production process is, ***there is one thing that all content production processes should have in common: Create content with a purpose and an audience in mind.*** The purpose of content marketing is to provide something educational, useful, or insightful to an audience. You need to know for whom you create the content, what to say to help them, and why you create the content. Needless to say, the tone-and-manner of content needs to reflect the essence

All content production process should create content with a purpose and an audience in mind.

of your brand. It's a universal rule of thumb for content marketing that content production should answer who, what, and why.

Having a global persona is important, but . . .

In the previous chapter, I recommended creating global personas and encouraged teams to collectively reach an agreement on which key target personas to focus. Once you start working on content with other regional teams, the audience question will continue to come up. Herein lies the challenge: regardless of what the teams agree to during the planning stage, the local teams may still make requests or decide to create content for different audiences. This has a lot to do with the requests coming from the local sales team, including local distributors and channel partners who are also your extended sales arms. They discover other sets of audiences they need to influence in order to close their sales.

I would like to clarify personas versus audiences in this case. An audience is generic and can cross multiple businesses. Examples include Millennials, sales representatives, or teachers. A global persona is a very specific cross-regional segment of an audience that we identify. For example: Business major in Ivy League college, Susan; IT manager in a major corporation, Joe. It takes resources and budget to create a persona and get everyone to agree. Local requests to focus on a specific audience do not mean you need to create a persona for it.

Reaching an agreement on personas and sticking to that agreement all the way through the process, from planning through promotion, may not be totally feasible, especially as some local marketing tactics or sales quotas may require fine tuning outside of the overall planning process. If the local teams need to focus on different sets of audiences, one of the 3 C's, Compromise, comes into play: acknowledge the differences as a team and determine alternative solutions. Sometimes it may be a Band-Aid approach, and that's OK, too. Here is one Band-Aid solution: Understand why the local team makes a request for different audiences. Make an effort to find common pain points and challenges between the global persona and new audience request. Resolve that request through reusing or making slight changes to existing content. Of course, you can create new and original content for the new audience, but the risk is that it takes away resources and focus from the existing personas.

It's common to create content for several personas. As I mentioned earlier, there are six consumer personas at Intel; Docusign has 20 personas worldwide. One cost-effective solution is to focus on common topics and write different versions for different personas.

Here's an example for a B2C scenario related to minivans: safety is a concern for soccer moms and working dads. One component of safety content can address how the airbag protects soccer moms' children, while another item of safety content could focus on the automatic braking feature intending to resonate better with the working dad's desire to protect his family. After all, deep down we all strive to be happy, productive, and provide what's needed to our families and our careers. The key is to find a way to connect your content to those desires.

For a B2B scenario: You may decide to create one horizontal-oriented content piece that targets sales executives of all industries. This same piece of content can be written differently to target sales executives in specific vertical segments such as manufacturing, financial institutions, publishing, construction, and others. You can also group some verticals together; for example, content for healthcare and insurance verticals can be similar without much revision.

Find a way to create several key pieces of content and stretch them across different personas.

Global content production must keep local needs in mind. Find a way to create several key pieces of content and stretch them across different personas. Even if the local teams need to deviate from the existing personas, there are still ways to solve the issues of focusing on different audiences. As long as both teams are committed, where there is a will, there will be a way.

Tips for global content production:

► Stick with agreed-upon global personas.

► Create content based on targeted common challenges or topics across multiple personas.

► Help the local team modify existing content for additional requests to suit different audiences.

Step 2: Learn from the Past

A key requirement, which tends to be overlooked during the content production process, is an understanding of the content landscape on our Web site. Here is the reason I recommend focusing on Web site, and not social media channels, other third-party communities, or paid-media properties: most companies have a hub and spoke model. It means that key content resides on the Web site. Any social media promotion or media marketing, ultimately, is intended to drive traffic back to the company Web site. Let's focus on understanding the content landscape of the Web site first, not your content on third-party sites. It may be important to know what content has been promoted and syndicated on other sites, but it's hard to gather content lists from external third-party sites. It's even harder to get the content performance from these external sites. Make an effort to comprehend your content inventory in your backyard first. Understanding the content landscape on your own Web site is time-consuming, but necessary.

Although global content production collaboration needs to be led by corporate, content audits need to be conducted at the regional and country level. The exception is the corporate site. Here is a perfect example: North America is a region of its own and the company is headquartered in the United States. Who owns the U.S. English site of a corporation? It varies from company to company. If the corporate site is also the U.S. site, it's usually managed by corporate.

Global content production collaboration needs to be led by corporate, content audits need to be conducted at the regional and country level.

However, I have seen co-ownership, where corporate and regional teams divide the ownership by pages. The leader for global content production can provide guidance and tools on how to conduct the audit, but the audit itself needs to happen locally. The findings and results should be shared by the local teams. If a local team doesn't have resources to do an audit, it's OK to conduct audits in only two or three languages, then the teams can draw insights from these sites.

A content audit is common when the online marketing team undergoes a major Web site redesign or content tool migration. It's like a house going through renovation. You need to go from room to room in the house to understand how the space is being used, and by whom, also noting what's not working and what's missing and needed. It's important to have *a sense* of the existing content list and tie it to specific target audiences. For big enterprises, there are hundreds and thousands of units of content on their Web sites. Don't get overwhelmed. You won't know them all. Narrow down your search to the relevant topics for targeting personas and key products. Talk to several content creators to understand what they have created. If they also blog and create different formats of content, read their blogs and their publications. Taking an inventory tells you not only what content you have, but also what types of content you have and the relationships and patterns within the content. Understanding the past with proper assessment helps you to determine what to produce in the future.

A quick content audit overview

Kristina Halvorson's *Content Strategy for the Web* shares a great overview of the content audit. She lists three types of content audit:

For what we've discussed to this point, the quantitative inventory audit makes sense. Depending on the volume of content on your Web site, your budget, and your time frame, you can sample from 10 percent to 100 percent of your content to understand what you have (see Figure 5.02). Sampling percentages depend on how in-depth you want to understand

CONTENT AUDIT IS A MUST

Audit Type	Description	When
Quantitative Inventory	A list of all or sample content you have— Just like the inventory of the products in a warehouse or store	Before content strategy work begins
Qualitative Audit: Best Practices Assessment	A comparison of your content against industry best practices— Usually done by a third party, unbiased assessor	Before strategy begins or in the early stages of strategy development
Qualitative Audit: Strategic Assessment	An in-depth look at how our content measures up to your strategic goals	Works best after your core strategy and key strategic recommendations are complete

Source: Content Strategy for the Web by Kristina Halvorson and Melissa Rach

FIGURE 5.02 Types of Content Audits

your past content and may also be a function of how extensive your Web site is. It's more efficient to use professional content audit tools and content management systems to pull the content information first, then merge or analyze the reports and get a sense of the overall content landscape.

If your company has a content management system (CMS), you may be able to gather the inventory from your CMS. There are also professional software tools to help you conduct a content audit such as Gather Content, Content Insight, Active Standards, Scrutiny, Screaming Frog and more.

Each tool offers slightly different features, so clearly articulating the key questions you would like to uncover with your audit will help you determine the right tool to use. Some typical questions to think about are—

Quantitative questions:

▶ How many content pieces are on your Web site? If your site is huge, you may scope it based on pages or topics.

▶ What are attributes of the data you find? The URLs, metadata, H1 text, links in and links out, and formats of content file types?

▶ Based on the sampling, can we classify content by our current editorial topics?

▶ Based on the sampling, can we map content to our target audience or personas?

Qualitative questions:

▶ What formats of content perform well?

▶ What content is e-mailed or shared by audiences?

▶ Is there any exclusive (locked or gated) content that requires customer information in order to download? How much?

▶ How does various gated content perform for lead generation?

▶ How technical is the content (beginning, intermediate, and advanced)?

▶ How can we map select existing content with a persona's purchase journey?

Using content inventory tools can certainly answer some of the above questions. Some will require you to pull data from other tools, and others will require you to do a lot of analysis of the content you pull. Throughout the audit, you will discover a lot of outdated content which needs to be retired. When you create content, it's also important to keep a shelf life of that content in mind. Some content management tools allow you to specify the end-of-life or refresh date for uploaded content. Having a shelf date for your content is a good way to set a reminder to refresh your content on a timely basis.

If specific local sites have a lot of content, I'd recommend the local team hire an agency or contractors to help them categorize the sampled content by personas, topics, and products.

Software can pull the reports for us, but the data itself has little value until it is analyzed. The more you understand your current content landscape, the better you are positioned to determine where gaps exist and what to create. Formulate your questions; buckle down to find your answers through tools, data analysis, and reading. There is no shortcut when you do a content audit. The whole process of reading, analyzing, gathering more information, and analyzing again can be incredibly boring. Yet, the lessons and findings you learn will be extremely beneficial for creating better content.

> *The more you understand your current content landscape, the better you are positioned to determine where gaps exist and what to create.*

What does sales enablement have to do with content marketing?

In addition to a content audit, there is another set of content you should be aware of: materials used to train and educate the sales team. It's called *sales enablement content.* In some industries and companies, the audiences we market to and the customers we sell to are two different segments. ***Our sales team may sell directly to distributors, dealers, resellers, software developers, solutions providers, retailers, and more, yet the marketing team markets to consumers or business users.*** Toyota sells their cars through their dealers to consumers. Toyota's direct sales team focuses on building relationships with dealers, yet Toyota marketing focuses on marketing to consumers. Coke does not sell Coke directly to consumers. They sell through extensive distribution channels. Coke's direct sales team focuses on building great relationships with various channels worldwide, yet Coke markets directly to consumers.

The mission of sales enablement for your sales partner is to transfer knowledge to your sales arms so they can effectively engage with customers and prospects. This is particularly important for B2B companies where the sales department needs to be educated regularly with new product roadmaps, features, and technologies before talking to customers. Through education and training, sales productivity increases as the amount of time and effort to find what sales people need decreases.

Granted, most sales enablement materials can be very technical and sales oriented, but these materials can still be great resources for content marketing. Sales enablement materials tend to focus on technical features, total cost comparisons, and are more training-centric, while marketing content focuses on end-user benefits, pricing, and offers. However, sales enablement content has changed dramatically, with some B2B companies moving away from product sales to more solution sales. The sales approach change also impacts the sales enablement materials. I have seen many sales enablement materials include end-user benefits, pricing and special offers. Sales enablement and end-user content have started to overlap more and more. You likely won't be able to use the material as is, but you can repurpose some sales training content into education-oriented content for your target personas.

Sales enablement and end-user content have started to overlap more and more.

Tips for global content production:

▶ Understand the overall content landscape by conducting an audit. Even if the audit is only done in one language on limited pages for specific personas, the team can still draw information from the content audit analysis.

▶ Conduct global content audits with the guidance, questions, and tools provided by corporate, but allow the execution and analysis to be done at the local level.

▶ Sales enablement materials need to be reviewed as part of the content audit.

Step 3: Here Comes Brainstorming

Once the content audit is completed, it's extremely useful to share the findings broadly with the key players who create, approve, and manage content. If everyone has some basic understanding about what content works well and what does not, it's much easier to move the team toward the next phase of deciding what content should be created. Learning from the past can help facilitate the brainstorming and discussion of what content we should create collectively to scale across different regions.

Every company manages brainstorming and discussions differently. For some companies, it's a daily get-together to discuss new ideas, report progress updates, and discuss any issues or challenges. This especially works well in an environment in which you need to publish content daily. In these frequent get-togethers, everyone knows the standing agenda and the standard drills. This is more of a newsroom approach, and can be done at corporate or local site. It's often location-based, where players tend to be in the same office to allow a quick huddle. Therefore, the global team's participation is likely to be limited. If you constantly refresh your Web site with daily news or updates, this approach makes sense.

For some companies, it's a one- or two-hour weekly meeting with sales (who know their customers well), subject matter experts (who know topics well), content creators, writing and design staff, and the local team. The goal for this type of meeting is to discuss potential content recommendations or refresh and repurpose old content pieces. During the weekly meeting, content creators also give updates on the pieces in progress. Some work-in-progress content is shared to solicit feedback. The local team has options to participate in the weekly meetings.

Some companies' content production processes are very campaign-driven. Content creation brainstorming sessions only happen when there are plans to run a big integrated campaign. It's not a regularly recurring meeting, but is more project focused.

The output of brainstorming is to come up with a list or rough titles of content to be produced for your personas. Some content pieces are no-brainers, such as any content related to your product and services. Some content requires discussion back and forth

The output of brainstorming is to come up with a list or rough titles of content to be produced for your personas.

on the format, story framework, and creative. If facilitated properly, the brainstorming session allows players to openly discuss any issues related to the content they are working on or bounce ideas off each other.

Daily huddles, weekly meetings, or campaign-driven get-togethers all have pros and cons. If you publish on a daily basis and multiple content pieces are in process at any given time, a daily huddle and weekly session are recommended. Campaign-driven brainstorming is very much project focused; it's hard to track from one campaign to another. If you want to create content marketing right and keep the content momentum going, having regular brainstorming sessions is the easiest way to tap into who is doing what and what has been done.

Step 4: Map Content Recommendations to Editorial Timelines

Out of the brainstorming and working sessions, a recommendation for the list of content to be produced, refreshed, or repurposed is created. Throughout periodic and continuous conversations, the list may continue to change. The list should be mapped to personas and products so the relevant players, such as the local teams, content creators, subject matter experts, lead generation, web marketing, and others, know what's coming. It's important to note that not all content pieces can be mapped to a product, but most of the content should be able to be mapped to personas. A company might create content about fitness and healthy diet for skiers, even though it sells ski boards or ski-related accessories. A software company might produce best practices for programmers, although its products are software development kits. In both of these examples, you're not necessarily tying the content to specific products, but you are aiming to be helpful to personas that fit into your target audience.

Create a timeline so that everyone is on the same page as to what will be produced, whom it's produced for, and when it will be completed. The production time of various content formats vary. Some content such as quick daily social media posts, third party content curation or weekly blog posts take little time with quick approvals. Some long form or campaign-oriented content requires four to six months of gathering information, writing with creative design, legal approvals, then localization and translation in order to scale to different countries. Jason Miller, LinkedIn's Global Content Marketing Manager, called it "Big Rock" content and I use the term, "Hero" content. Miller's approach is to create a Big Rock content every four to six months, then use that piece to create different formats of content such as webcasts, e-books, multiple blogs, and videos. In addition to different formats, Miller goes one step further and customizes the Big Rock content for different verticals. Refer to LinkedIn's case study at the end of the chapter.

While collaborating with creative designers, webmasters, copy writers and other team members, it's more efficient to use project management tools to map content to personas and products while using the same tools to track the progress of different content production. You can use project management tools such as Microsoft Project, Trello, Basecamp, or Kapost to keep everyone marching to the same beat.

Step 5: Identify Owners to Create Content from Within Content

Content creators can exist inside or outside of the company. If they are inside the company, they can also be at the corporate level or in regions and countries. There are three models:

- ► In-house
- ► Outsourcing
- ► Hybrid

In-house staff

Some companies have in-house staff responsible for content creation. Topics are assigned to them. They interview subject matter experts, research the topics, and then write and produce the content. They may also have in-house layout, design, and video production staff. Big enterprises, or companies that publish often, typically have capabilities set up in-house.

The in-house staff may support not only corporate content, but also work with the regional and local teams on their content.

Outsourced to agencies and freelancers

In some companies, content creators are program managers who manage content to be produced by agencies or freelancers. One person acts as a conduit between subject matter experts and agencies or freelancers. This person also monitors the overall progress of content creation. This process tends to work well for smaller companies who leverage various agencies and freelancers whenever content needs to be created.

Hybrid model

The hybrid model means the work is divided between internal and external resources; perhaps the content is written by in-house staff, but the design and layout is done externally or vice versa. The hybrid model is the one most commonly used. Even for big enterprises, there may not be in-house staff at the regional and country level. If the region and country teams would like to create content, they may go to agencies or freelancers. At the corporate level, it's fully in-house, yet outside the headquarters a hybrid model is used.

In the past, the content creator was responsible for one piece of content at a time. To keep local's needs and multi-channel efforts in mind, it's now more efficient and effective to create different content formats. For example, a 20-page e-book can be repurposed into two or three infographics, one SlideShare presentation, and five or six customized images for Facebook, Twitter, and other social media posts. Create content from within content. Proactively think through how this content will be promoted or used. At this stage, it is also important to get the local team's feedback. At the regular sync meeting between headquarters and local, share what content is coming.

Create content from within content. Proactively think through how this content will be promoted or used.

The local team can also provide some feedback on how they will use the content and give the content creators ideas on how to create content from within content. The key thing is not to focus on producing just one piece of content, but to give some advance thought as to whether or not the content can be morphed or repurposed into different formats. At this stage it's also fitting to give some thought to extracting quotes and stats from content for social media usage. For instance, tweeting teasers on Twitter may lead potential consumers to your web presence.

The major disadvantages of creating content from within content are costs and production time. The cost of content production will go up, especially if most of your content is outsourced to agencies and freelancers. Also, it may extend the content completion deadline. By the way, you don't need to do content within content for every single piece of content. Focus on a couple of "Hero" content (Big Rock) pieces that you know the headquarters and local teams will promote heavily or use in specific campaigns.

Step 6: Project Management from Creation to Publication

Using spreadsheets to track the list of content and its progress is one solution. But it won't cut it for bigger efforts, especially if a high volume of content is being generated and involves in-house writing staff, designers, external agencies, and possibly the local teams. More and more companies are exploring tools to automate the content production processes. The Content Marketing Institute created a 49-page guide detailing 13 technology solutions for powering content marketing (bit.ly/toolforcontent). Some of the solutions focus on editorial project management and search engine optimization. Some focus on content production collaboration from idea generation to completion, while other tools focus on tapping into a writers' network. These tools are still new and evolving. Each tool has its niche and can help you simplify the content production processes. The challenge is to understand your requirements and to choose the one that fits your needs.

Step 7: Publish the Content for Others to Access

When the content is done, it needs to be uploaded to a content management tool or database so others can access it. Sometimes, the finished content will be published directly to the corporate Web site first. It can then be used as a template and localized or translated so it can be deployed to other countries and regions.

Step 8: Sharing Content with the Local Teams

If the local teams are deeply integrated with the content production process, it's good to share the content as it's created.

> *The structured approach is to create a content kit, putting together a list of content as a kit. Categorize the content by editorial topics and personas.*

Instead of sharing one piece of content at a time with multiple countries, it's more efficient to share a set of content on a regular basis, perhaps on a monthly or a quarterly basis. The structured approach is to create a content kit, putting together a list of content as a kit. Categorize the content by editorial topics and personas. Give a description and hyperlink or file share location for each content piece. The following information is incorporated into a kit:

- ▶ Editorial calendar
- ▶ A short description of topical story framework and messaging
- ▶ Keyword search recommendations
- ▶ Top five content recommendations by personas
- ▶ A list of detailed content by product or purchase journey

Work with the local teams on localization and translation. Some content can be easily translated, while some will require customization and/or translation. Ultimately, the purpose of a content kit is to allow each region and country team to understand what content is available for them to use. Based on the kit, they can determine if there is a content gap they need to close with locally created content.

Something to Consider for Content Production

Quality versus Quantity

In a perfect world, we hope to churn out great quality content in the optimal quantity that our audience will consume. We are all inspired to create content that will make our customer say: "I didn't know that" or "that was cool, let me share it." In reality, "great" quality content takes time to produce and "optimal" quantity is an unknown and situational. It's not easy to create high-quality content day in and day out.

> *"Great" quality content takes time to produce and optimal quantity is unknown. It's not easy to consistently create high-quality content.*

The purpose of content is to educate, help, challenge, or entertain. With the rise of social media, we want our audiences to share and like our content. Ultimately, the end goal is to drive sales of our products and services, while being helpful to our customers.

If I need to pick one or the other, I would focus on quality. Content marketing works if you have something meaningful to say that the audience will find educational, beneficial, and insightful. I am also cognizant that regular and frequent communications are important to keep your brand and products front and center in your audience's mind. Again, it comes back to the point I made earlier: create content with a purpose. What do you want to accomplish with the content you want to create? Don't create for the sake of creating content. Focus on how you can help the audience; the rest will take care of itself.

Is the Purchase Funnel Still Valid for Content Production?

In 1898, Elias St. Elmo Lewis created the modern concept of the purchase funnel. He divides consumer interest and behavior into four stages (AIDA)[2]:

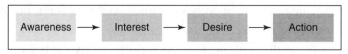

The stages have been modified many different ways depending on industry, marketing channel, or audience. Andrew Chak, in his book, *Submit Now: Designing Persuasive Web Sites*, suggests the Web site or landing page should be designed to correspond to the AIDA stage.

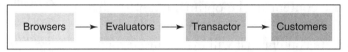

You may have seen this as a version that includes sell-up and post sale support:

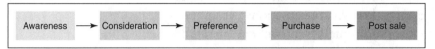

If you search the Internet for "purchase channel or purchase funnel," you can see various versions of the purchase funnel framework with different stages being added or modified. But the core concept of a purchase cycle stays the same: your customer recognizes they have an issue or a need. You have a product or service to address their issue or satisfy their need, but they don't know about it. You market your product or service to make sure people are aware of it. Because customer issues need to be resolved or their needs have to be fulfilled, they do research and discover your products (try to make it easy for them). They become interested in what you have to offer. Then, they evaluate multiple options, if any, and eventually make a purchase decision based on the information available to them at the time they're ready to buy.

In theory, the purchase funnel is pretty linear and straightforward. After the rise of the Internet and search engines, the customer's purchase behavior is all over the place, going up and down the purchase funnel. The customer's purchase journey "looks less like a funnel and more like a flight map" according to Google's Zero Moment of Truth (ZMOT) Handbook.[3] Through constant searching and content consumption using their mobile devices, customers bounce back and forth between awareness, consideration, and evaluation stages at any given time using multiple different touch points. Buying is a process involving starts and stops, resets, reevaluations and adjustments. Looking from the sideline, it may be hard for marketers to make sense of a customer's journey, but it's logical from the lenses of customers. For instance, a customer may download awareness-oriented content from your Web site, then immediately consume a product deployment guide that provides an indication that this customer may be ready to make

> *The purchase funnel is linear, yet our purchasing behavior is not.*

a purchase. But no purchase is made at that time. Then three weeks later they return and consume several product introduction videos. ***This going back and forth, hopping in and out of the purchase stages, is how we shop now. The purchase funnel is linear, yet our purchasing behavior is not.*** As part of content creation planning, it still makes sense to create content for the different stages of the purchase funnel. However, it does not make sense to map content to customers' multiple touchpoint purchase behaviors, since everyone's purchase journey is different. In a way, mapping content to customers' purchase behaviors is a content placement and promotion discussion. We may never know exactly how each customer reaches a decision to buy our products and services, but we should have a basic understanding of where our customers usually go to search and consume our content or any content for similar products and services. Take the content to where customers go.

Format of Content Is Irrelevant to the Purchase Journey

Some content marketers map different formats of content to different stages of the purchase funnel. For example, banner ads work best at the awareness stage, while case studies are most useful at the consideration and preference stages. Mapping content types or formats to a purchase funnel limits your creative approach. ***The way to map content to the purchase cycle is to ensure you deliver the appropriate information to your target customers at each stage,*** not ***by content format or type.***

Depending on how you tell your story, a video format can be appropriate for the awareness or evaluation or even postpurchase stages. You can use a video to introduce your product, which is awareness. You can also use a video to demonstrate the features and capability comparison of your and your competitors' products, which is for the consideration stage. In addition, you can use video to show how to upgrade after purchase. Video is a format that works throughout the different stages of a purchase funnel. Don't map content types to the purchase journey. Map what information you want to deliver throughout the purchase journey. Determine what you want to deliver and communicate first. The form will come later.

And the opposite is also true. I spoke with Doug Kessler, creative director of Velocity, a United Kingdom-based content marketing agency, and he stressed that it's also appropriate to pick a format first, and then determine how you want to tell a story. *The key to keep in mind is to deliver useful information to your personas*.

Constantly Consuming Content Means Constantly Evaluating

Today, all sort of reviews, product comparisons, and educational techniques are available to potential customers at almost no cost; people consume content all the time. Itamar Simonson and Emanuel Rosen, in their book *Absolute Value*, call out an interesting phenomenon: sophisticated consumers don't research technologies or products when they need them. "Some people don't see the need to postpone information acquisition until a specific purchase intention is formed."[4] They track and follow products and technology on a regular basis. Simonson and Rosen nicknamed this continuing information acquisition process "couch tracking," "like sports buffs keeping track of the game from their couches."[5] That's why gadget Web sites such as Gizmodo and Engadget get millions of views each month. More and more consumers are continually following specific topics that are of interest to them, even though they may not be in the market for a purchase at the time.

It's very interesting that Simonson, Rosen, and I reached a similar conclusion from different points of view. In Chapter 1, I shared my observation that good content is readily available at almost no cost and our smartphones serve as an instant gateway to access that knowledge base and our social desire to connect with others. Since we are so attached to our phones, we can't help but check messages, stay connected, or frequently consume content on our favorite Web sites and social networks. I use the term *chase content*, while Simonson and Rosen use the term *couch tracking*. Either way, it means that preferences are often formed well in advance of purchase intent. Instead of focusing on ready-to-buy consumers, Simonson and Rosen argue that marketers should focus on the couch trackers and communicate with them before they form their opinions. Because our customers are constantly reading and searching, we need to think differently about the types of content we create and syndicate. A customer's continual content consumption behavior is a great opportunity for brands to change their brand perception or attributes using relevant content.

> *Chase content and couch tracking mean preferences are often formed well in advance of purchase intent.*

Creating Content with Minimal Localization and Translation

Video or images are two formats that can often be reused without localization and translation. Two perfect examples of a single video that can scale to other countries without much customization are P&G's Olympics "Thank you, Mom" commercial (bit.ly/thxmoms) and Logitech's New Office/Home Office video (bit.ly/dinnermeet).

Although Logitech's dinner setting may resonate more with small business owners in developed countries, you "get" what they want to convey without localization or translation. These two videos made a lasting impression on audiences. P&G's example casts moms and kids from multiple countries;

in a way, it's a global video. Logitech's video focuses on small business owners. In that video, there is no dialogue, yet you understand the pains and challenges of small business owners. Both videos focus on storytelling and emotional connections first, then weave the products into the story in an organic way. P&G's commercial does not even mention products and only shows the product brands at the end of the commercial. Yet, we all remember it's a P&G commercial.

Although P&G's video reflects local living environments and cultural nuances, Logitech's video does not heavily identify with any specific location or culture. However, both story frameworks are understood by their target audiences, regardless of where they live. It's possible to create content without much customization and localization if you really take the time to pinpoint scenarios that highlight your audience's pain points and present the solution in a very human, simple, and universal way.

Words are not Dead

Words carry weight. Words have the power to motivate or demoralize, to reward or condemn, when the right combination is used. Words matter for marketing, especially content marketing. Creative and visual matter, too, but the words you choose will channel your audience's emotion and influence their decision-making process.

> Words carry weight. Words have the power to motivate or demoralize, to reward or condemn, when the right combination is used.

Georgia Tech researchers Eric Gilbert and Tanushree Mitra published a research paper, "The Language that Gets People to Give: Phrases that Predict Success on Kickstarter." A lot of factors influence the odds of a project achieving its funding goals: the name of your project, dollar amount, project duration, products and/or services, the category of your project, the intention of your project, and even the format of your show-and-tell videos. Gilbert and Mitra asked: Does the language used by a project creator play a major role in driving the success of reaching funding goals? Do the words you choose influence people's desire to give?

Kickstarter is a crowd funding Web site. It's a platform for artists and entrepreneurs to raise funds from the general public. In about four years since its launch in 2009, five million people have pledged over $1 billion for more than 60,000 creative projects.[6] Project creators set a funding goal and deadline. If people like the project, they can pledge the money to make it happen. It's astoundingly effective in rallying people around an idea. Project creators must reach their funding goal to receive the funds from Kickstarter. Approximately 44 percent of projects have reached their funding goals.[7]

Gilbert and Mitra studied "a corpus of 45,000 crowd-funded projects, analyzed 9 million phrases and 59 other variables commonly present on crowd funding sites."[8] One of the key findings is that "the language used in the project has surprising predictive power—accounting for 58.56 percent of the variance around successful funding."[9] In other words, if you use certain phrases and words, it encourages people to pledge and enhances your chance to achieve your funding goals.

They identified the top 100 phrases that signal likely success in funding. Here are some of the phrases that signal the project will be funded:

"project will be"

"also receive two"

"and encouragement"

"given the chance"

"a personal tour"

They also shared the top 100 phrases that are associated with projects that will *not* get funded:

"not been able"

"we have lots"

"provide us"

"the needed"

"the profits"

The research concluded that phrases used in successful Kickstarter campaigns exhibit general persuasion principles. "Those campaigns that follow the concept of reciprocity—that is, offer a gift in return for a pledge—and the perceptions of social participation and authority, generated the greatest amount of funding."[10] Perhaps unsurprisingly, the successful projects use words to demonstrate a sense of confidence, future success, social participation, and special offers with backers in mind. The research controlled 59 variables and was able to validate one point: Word selection matters. Some words resonate with backers more than others and persuade them to give.

> Word selection matters. Some words resonate with backers more than others and persuade them to give.

In content marketing, it's important to understand what words resonate with your audience based on their pain points, challenges, and needs. To scale content across other countries, it's necessary to localize or translate as you see fit. Use social listening, search engine marketing (SEM), A/B testing on your Web sites and media buys, or use focus group testing to test various keywords and optimize based on their performance.

Coexistence: Original Content and Curated Content

Original content is the content you create, e.g. your blog post, your webinar, your e-book, etc. Curated content is created by others and may be acquired or commissioned and then shared on your site or social media channels. *In the "create" stage, we focus on original content. In the promote stage, you should mix original and curated content*. Pick and choose the relevant content from third party sources you know your customers will enjoy. There are some tools out there such as Curata, PublishThis, ContentGem, Scoop.it, and Trap!t, which can help you select content for your audience.

In general, original content tends to perform better than curated content. Original content is best for driving SEO traffic and social sharing, but it takes time, resources and budget to create. Curation can be equally good at establishing thought leadership and engagement while providing the advantage of content freshness in less time and at a reduced cost.[11] Curated content can't replace original content, but it's certainly a great complement and another option for your editorial planning if you have limited time and budget. Carefully curated content can also be used for your e-mail and newsletters, if the content is informational in nature and provides insights.

It makes sense for the headquarters to recommend content curation tools, yet content curation can be done globally or locally. It's best if the local teams pick and choose what matters to their local audiences. If the curated content is selected globally, the annotation of the content needs to be done locally to add the proper local context. Content curation can be done with the help of agencies as well.

Creative and User Experience Design

Creative and design play a major role in your web and mobile app's appeal and ability to effectively present content. Your brand guide, visual and writing style playbooks determine the creative development, look-and-feel and tone-and-manner of your content. *Know what your brand stands for. Know who you are.*

Layout also plays an important role in helping an audience navigate through Web sites on both desktop and mobile devices to find useful content. The design can be beautiful, but if the content is not useful you will not achieve your goals. Similarly, the content can be great, but if it's difficult to find on your Web site, it can lead to a frustrating and negative experience for the target audience.

Should content come first or should design or layout of an app or Web site come first? It's a chicken or egg question. Ultimately, the content you create needs to go somewhere. It can go on your Web site or on a third-party Web site, it can be online or print, and it can be used for internal employee or customer facing communications. The important task is to determine where you want to place your content before creating it. You do not need to know every channel where you would like to syndicate your content, but you need to have a general idea of the primary channels where the content will be showcased or used.

Most of the time, the content creator, app designer, web master and web designer are different people. It's important that designers and content creators talk to each other. Content creators should understand the design and layout of apps, web pages, and print. It will give you a sense of the format of content you should create to complement the design. Design is the house itself; content is all the furniture and accessories for the house. In order to create an experience, both design and content are equally important. That's why creating content for multiple channels can be pretty challenging. One possible solution is to create content as component parts (or modules) that can be appropriately assembled for multiple formats. This requires content creators to think and structure content differently, and it also needs to have tools to support the module approach of different content pieces.

> *We should give advance thought as to which are the primary channels where we should place that content.*

There is no way we can completely figure out which content should go where, but we should give advance thought as to which are the primary channels where we should place that content. Take into account the user experience and web design and layout.

In Summary

Every company has a different content creation process. Understand what works for you and your team. The local team's input is part of the global content creation process. Make sure that the local team is included in the process. Create content with a sense of purpose and a persona in mind. Content creation can be a messy, creative process. Idea generation, writing, format, and layout changes can all happen simultaneously. Embrace the messiness. Something good usually comes out of it.

Here is the dilemma that you need to comprehend and manage when you create content. When the audience searches, it expect answers. Yet, to make your content stand out, you need to give them more than just the answer. You should give them a straight answer, yet you should also give them something they don't know. **Pablo Picasso said, "Computers are useless. They can only give you answers."**[12] **When you create content, give them insights beyond just answers.**

Content creation can be a messy, creative process. Idea generation, and layout changes can all happen simultaneously. Embrace the messiness.

For Entrepreneurs and Small Businesses Owners

▶ The best way to grow your audience is to provide useful content, even if some content is not directly related to your products or services.

▶ Budget is a major concern. You may need to DIY. There is no shortcut.

▶ Really zoom in to solve your customer's issues and help them.

For Enterprise Marketing Managers

▶ Create content with local team's feedback in mind.

▶ Build a content creation process to brainstorm and manage content progress.

▶ Communicate final content pieces with the local team through a content kit.

For Agencies and Marketing Consultants

▶ Don't just help your client create only primary content, instead help them to determine how they can create content from within content.

- ▶ Guide your clients to think through content placement strategies to help determine the appropriate content and formats to develop.
- ▶ Help them write the same piece of content for different personas.

CASE STUDY

LinkedIn's "Big Rock" Content

One out of three professionals on the planet has an account on LinkedIn.[13] When we are promoted, search for jobs or look for peer connections, LinkedIn is the first place we stop. As of April 18th, 2014, the total number of LinkedIn users reached 300M[14] representing 200 countries and territories.[15] Twenty-six languages are available on LinkedIn as of October 23rd, 2013.[16] It's a true global community. LinkedIn's content pages receive six times more views than their job pages.[17] Content is king.

LinkedIn has three major business lines: the Talent Solutions Group, the Marketing Solutions Group and the Premium Subscription Group. The Talent Solution Group offers services to the LinkedIn Recruiters. The Marketing Solutions Group offers content marketing and advertising services and products, while the Premium Subscription Group offers premium access subscription services to LinkedIn members. Each group manages its marketing efforts differently.

I had the pleasure of talking with Jason Miller, Global Content Marketing Manager for the Marketing Solutions Group. His content production approach is "Big Rock, Small Rock." His small rock is the frequent posts on LinkedIn's Marketing Solutions Blog, while his Big Rock is long-form content (a presentation, an e-book, a video, etc.) packed with valuable content and visually compelling creative and design. Unlike daily blog posts, this takes time, resource and budget. When he started his job with the Marketing Solutions Group, Miller cataloged the features and benefits of all his division's products in an 80-page document. Using the information he collected, he created a beautiful and well-crafted e-book: *The Sophisticated Marketer's Guide to LinkedIn*.[18] I remember seeing the e-book and thinking to myself: "this is a great piece of content." It caught my attention and I avidly read through the whole e-book.

Initially, Miller only shared this on LinkedIn and received 12,000 downloads without any promotion. As a sophisticated content marketer, he then took this e-book and repurposed it in multiple different formats such as infographics, short blog posts, podcasts, a SlideShare presentation, physical books and webinars. These different formats use the same look-and-feel to ensure creative consistency. Then, he promoted these snackable short content pieces using various communications channels such as Twitter, LinkedIn InMail, e-mail, display ads, guest blogs, sponsored updates and more.

The story does not end there. He took it globally and shared this content with his regional and country teams. His counterparts in other regions localized and translated it. With his 80-page source document, he started creating a series from the *Sophisticated Guide* for different verticals and audience segments such as *the Sophisticated Marketer's Guide to LinkedIn – Finance Edition, the Sophisticated Marketer's Guide to Thought Leadership on LinkedIn.* He continues to build on his original content using the same theme but tailoring the material for very specific audiences. It's amazing how creative Miller is in repurposing and repackaging his Big Rock.

CASE STUDY

How Much Content Can Vology Create with $1,000?

This case study is not about global content creation, per se, yet I feel compelled to share it with you. It's about a marketing manager in a small business with a small budget that finds creative ways to create content. Certain aspects of this approach still align with the processes mentioned in this chapter. She still has informal editorial topics, uses various freelancers to help her, and manages the production process by herself. It shows how resilient we can be even with a limited budget.

A tight budget does not make it impossible to create content. I met Debi Steigerwald, digital marketing director at Vology, at a conference. Through a casual conversation with Steigerwald, I discovered her budget for content creation is $1,000 a month. Yes, *only $1,000 to create original content*. I was intrigued and asked her how she does it.

Her company, Vology, offers complete IT services and solutions for SMB and larger enterprises. Like many other IT service providers, they are also a certified channel partner with companies like Intel, Dell, Acer, Cisco, Juniper, Citrix, Microsoft, RiverBed, and other solution providers. As a value-added reseller (VAR) and SMB, Vology competes heavily with other IT service providers and their profit margin can be thin. It makes sense to me that Steigerwald's content budget is tight.

I asked how she manages her $1,000 per month. Here is what she shared with me:

► Leverage free content from partners and manufacturers: Vology is a certified partner that sells hardware, software, or services for more than 30 solution providers and manufacturers. Those companies provide ample content for their channel partners, like Vology, to enable them to sell and market to their customers.

Steigerwald takes their partners' content (and it is *free*) and cobrands key content with Vology's logo and contact information. In this way, she creates semioriginal content without spending any money.

► Reuse content as much as possible:
  Vology hosts a two-day annual event for their customers. A lot of useful content is created for the event: keynotes, videos and audios, speaker presentations, print collaterals, and others.

She reuses these content pieces for tradeshows, events, the Vology Web site, and other marketing channels throughout the year.

► Repackage content into digestible and snackable pieces:
  Steigerwald uses Fiverr, Tenrr, and other sites to find affordable freelancers. According to Steigerwald, she would send a rough cut of a 45-minute video to an offshore video editor. She makes sure that she provides very specific directions on how to edit the video and suggests the opening and closing. She can get someone to edit the video for $15. Then, she will send the same video to another person to do the sound track for another $15. White board video is another creative way to create a quick and easy video.

For example, her CEO did a 3-minute video explaining its unique business model to prospects and customers. Steigerwald provided a short script, product images, and usages along with that video to a freelancer. The result was a short 2-minute white board video for $150. It took only four days.

She also outsources copywriting and blogs. She makes sure she uses native English speakers. Through trial-and-error, she eventually finds writers to fit her needs. Then, she gives the writers specific guidance and educates them on her products. Ultimately, she has several writers that she can tap into for product descriptions and blog posts.

Here are some tips:

Provide specific directions: Working with offshore freelancers, it's vital to provide "crisp" and "specific" directions. You need to clearly understand what you are looking for from the get-go. The more specific the direction, the better outcome you receive.

Do more than your share: With limited budget, Steigerwald writes short scripts, does research on topics for blogs, understands video and audio editing, runs keyword searches, and so on. You need to get your hands dirty when your budget is tight. Hustle!

Be creative: Steigerwald took senior managers' headshots and found a freelancer to hand draw each senior manager's image for $10 each. She used the hand drawn images for presentations and received great feedback. Creativity *is* affordable.

Think differently and work the best you can with the budget and resources you have.

CHAPTER SIX

The Third P of the Global Content Marketing Cycle: Promote

Definition of Promote:

Promote is to establish a market-driven content distribution process with paid and social media. Publish the appropriate formats of content with the optimal frequency in targeted channels. Use tools and data to optimize the media buy and social media content distribution.

> *"If a tree falls in a forest and no one is around to hear it, does it make a sound?"*
>
> **—UNKNOWN**

Promotion Is More Than Half the Battle

Ask any writers or musicians, and they will tell you that promoting their work is harder than creating it. Creating compelling content is only half of the battle; the other half (actually more than half) is to get your awesome content out where your target audience can stumble upon it. Doug Kessler jokingly stresses the importance of content promotion in his "Diary of a Content Pimp" blog series: "Somewhere between 42 and 67 percent of the success of a given piece of content comes down to the quality, relevance and timeliness of the piece itself. (Source: Fictional Research Associates, Ltd). The rest is down to how hard you work to get your shiny new piece of content out there. . . . ."[1] In the world of content marketing, if you post some collateral on a tree in a forest where no one is around to see it, from the perspective of measuring the impact of content, you might as well not have spent the money and time to create that content in the first place.

> *Promotion is about placing your content so it's appropriately accessible to the target audience.*

In general, the word *promotion* has a negative connotation. Promoting your content does not mean screaming at your audience. It does not mean interrupting your customers, either. Or if you do want to scream or interrupt your audience, please scream at them politely or interrupt them tactfully. I have to admit that screaming and interrupting may still work at times if it's done intelligently. But generally, promotion is about placing your content so it's appropriately accessible to the target audience.

There Is No "Free" Promotion

Everything has a price tag. Your time is worth something; you either pay with your time or your money. You can promote your content for "free" on Twitter. Twitter itself is free, but the time and effort to tweet relentlessly every hour of every day is not free. Hiring someone to think of catchy material for your tweets is not free. Facebook is free to use. But if you really want to reach a broader audience, you have to pay to generate awareness. Otherwise, very limited numbers of people will see your content, unless you get very lucky. In some ways, some social media channels are becoming more and more like paid media channels and less like "earned" media from the perspective of their advertising-driven business models. You have to either pay with your money or your time or both. When it gets down to brass tacks, for promotion, you need to pay your dues. There is really no such thing as a free lunch.

Different Types of Content Promotions

There are "big" and "small" promotional efforts. Big and small do not necessarily imply big or small budgets. It can refer to budget, or it can also refer to the intensiveness of the time and effort that we will spend to plan and execute a promotion.

Promotions also can be worldwide or country driven. Corporate and local do not need to run the same campaigns simultaneously all the time, yet it's important to have an understanding of what the corporate and local teams will promote collectively and what will be worked on individually. For big product launches or major corporate announcements, it makes sense to coordinate the promotional efforts between the corporate and local teams. Even for daily social media content promotion, it's helpful to know what other countries are doing. Sometimes it's more efficient to borrow with pride by using or quickly adapting another country's content, as long as you have the appropriate rights. Celebration of a new year or a new seasonal change can easily work across countries, if copy or images focus on seasonal changes, health, or happiness. How each country promotes its not their content can be a great standing topic to discuss at the headquarters and local sync meetings.

Content promotion is not all about promotional budget, although it does help. It's about spending the time and effort to carefully and thoughtfully integrate varieties of paid, earned, and owned media, wherever and whenever it makes sense.

Traditional promotional programs place more emphasis on paid media, public relations (PR), and broadcast media coverage. With the rise of social media, modern promotional programs focus on using organic, creative, and long tail promotional efforts. If you don't have a large budget, your promotional effort needs to be creative and compel others to spread your messages for you.

Although there are more, here are some types of promotions for global content marketing:

- ▶ Content promotion as part of major launches or corporate announcements
- ▶ Special and targeted promotion for hero or flagship content pieces
- ▶ Routine content promotion of daily blogs and regularly featured content
- ▶ Limited time offer promotions

Regardless of the types of promotions, it's important to identify a clear call-to-action for your audience. For product launches, your call-to-action may be "contact your sales representative" or "free trial" of your new products. For daily blogs and regularly featured content, it can be "subscribe to newsletters" or "special promotions." Your content is a means through which your audience can act.

Content Promotion as Part of Major Launches:

Depending on the type of launch, content can play a critical role. If a keynote is given by the CEO, the presentation can be uploaded as a video to the company's Web site and YouTube for your audience to view. The video is also a perfect complement to the press release, which makes it easy for a press pickup. A short video or solutions brief can be produced to educate the target audience about new enhanced product benefits and features with the call-to-action of "buy now" or "contact your sales representative." An e-mail campaign about "what's new" can be sent to subscribers and prospects with limited time offers. Understand the launch plan and help the launch manager or coordinator connect the dots through content promotions designed to complement that plan.

How to scale globally: Regardless of the size of a company, product launches are usually done in multiple markets within a short period of time. The oversight for launch content and creative development is usually driven from the corporate office, after which local and country teams will translate the content and promote it as part of local launches. Depending on the scope of a cross-regional launch, it can take a huge amount of coordination to execute effectively. To do this well, regular headquarters and local sync meetings are absolutely essential. A leader needs to be identified to coordinate with the local teams. Roles and responsibilities and a clear timeline are mapped out and communicated. Overcommunication is better than undercommunication when working with the team across countries.

Special and Targeted Promotion for Hero Content

If you spend a great deal of money and effort to create flagship or hero content, you need to spend an equal amount of time and effort to promote it. Examples of flagship content are extensive research reports, future trends, your company's leadership point of view, or even a complete guide of something such as Social Media Today's 2014 Social Customer Engagement Index: Exclusive Whitepaper,[2] IBM's Global CMO Study,[3] Intel's Big Data 101,[4] and Google's Mobile Playbook.[5] Flagship or hero content communicates interesting insights or additional know-how that can benefit your audience. It makes sense to put budget, time, and effort into creating a promotional plan to market the flagship content.

How to scale globally: If it's true hero content, there should be no question that the corporate and local teams must collaborate from the outset. The local teams are involved prior to the production of the content to ensure that it is being scaled. As a result, marketing engines at headquarters and local teams are committed to doing whatever it takes to extend the life of this content. However, I have seen some exceptions in which the flagship content was created at headquarters without much of the local teams' engagement. This usually happened when the content needed to be created in a compressed timeline. Then, the local teams will take the flagship content as-is and modify it to add local flavor. The local team has the full right to decide which key content they would like to promote. This is not ideal, if you truly aim to scale flagship content globally.

Routine Content Promotion of Daily Blogs and Regularly Featured Content

These are promotion efforts you do for your daily or weekly blogs, YouTube videos, Facebook, Instagram, and social media posts. It's the content that you generate or curate on a regular basis to keep the engagement going with your target audience.

How to scale globally: In general, it's challenging for headquarters to manage daily content for social media in various different countries in different languages. Some social media platforms such as Facebook, allow the headquarters or an agency to manage country-specific pages or one global page to be posted in different countries for different audiences. If you are looking to promote flagship content in a more integrated manner at the local level, it's best to have the local team take the lead for planning and implementation. Headquarters provides content and the local teams can pick and choose the best items to use in the most appropriate channels. For example, the corporate blog can be translated and customized with a local perspective. If you also curate third-party content, it's better to draw upon local resources. Daily content promotion needs to be owned and managed by the local team with agreed-upon objectives and metrics.

Limited Time Offer Promotions

Tie content marketing to limited time offers. Due to taxes, laws, regulations, as well as supply and demand, offers or special promotions are usually localized. Contests, drawings, apps, or content downloads and other engaging activities can be used to entice your customers to participate. A contest can be used to encourage users to share your content or create

THE THIRD P OF GLOBAL CONTENT MARKETING: PROMOTE [**133**

user-generated content to win prizes, for example. This type of effort is not routine and recurring, but content can certainly play a role in promotional campaigns by encouraging contestants to try your products, download exclusive content or apps, or interact with your messages through games or quizzes.

How to scale globally: It's very inefficient to run a contest with prizes across two or more countries, even just the United States and Canada, without involving the local teams. However, it's beneficial to share any innovative offer-oriented content promotions between regions or countries. This can also be a standing topic for the regular headquarters and local sync meetings.

Four-Step Content Promotional Process

Regardless of the types of content promotion, here is a process to help you create a content promotion plan (see Figure 6.01).

Step 1: Establish Promotional Objectives and Measurements

Depending on the different types of content promotion, you need to determine your promotional objectives. Does the content aim to generate leads? How many? Is the content part of a launch to drive sales through limited offers? What are projected sales? Your promotional objectives and measurements need to tie back to the global content marketing objectives you would like to accomplish.

Depending on the different types of content promotion, you need to determine your promotional objectives.

Any promotion plan needs to be developed with the purpose of achieving business objectives. In addition to aligning with business objectives, promotional objectives should also relate to call-to-action of your promotions or campaigns.

Step 2: Allocate Budget (if any) and Brainstorm Promotional Ideas

Determine if there is budget to support the promotional activities. Usually launches, limited offers, and hero or flagship

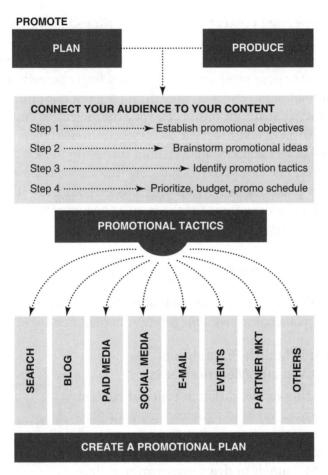

FIGURE 6.01 Four-Step Content Promotional Process

content will have a budget for promotions. For launches or limited offer promotions, a campaign theme may be needed to grab customers' attention and generate interest. For routine or targeted flagship content promotion at a local level, which tends not to be well funded, focus on brainstorming creative and catchy campaigns to coordinate various free promotional platforms.

Step 3: Identify and Prioritize Promotional Tactics

Over time we develop an arsenal of promotional tactics that we tend to use. The key is to prioritize which tactics to dial up.

At this step, we also need to understand the list of content and the associated formats for the list of content. Understand what content is available and map different formats of content into different promotional channels to build your promotional plan.

Here are some examples of content promotional tactics:

Search

Hopefully, before the content is completed, keywords and phrases used in the content have been properly researched and aligned with the topic. The search part of the promotion is to ensure that you have done all the basics so the content can be easily discovered (titles, tags, URL, metadata, etc.). A basic step of content promotion is to ensure that your content is searchable and ranks high organically. Don't focus on just search algorithms; aim at creating good quality content your audience will enjoy and incorporate appropriate search key phrases.

> *Don't focus on just search algorithms; aim at creating good quality content your audience will enjoy and incorporate appropriate search key phrases.*

How to scale globally: If the content is localized and translated, the keywords for local languages may need to be adjusted or created. Usually, delivering a list of keywords to the local team along with the finished content helps them determine a list of keywords to use. If ad word bidding is involved, there is merit for the headquarters to centralize the bid so that each country does not bid up the price.

Blog

If your company has a blog, write several different posts talking about flagship content, product launch highlights, and limited offers to build a long tail effect.

How to scale globally: Blogging takes a lot of time and effort; not all local teams can afford to do blogging in a sustained manner, even if the local team hires freelancers to do it. With external freelancers, the local team still needs to spend time to proofread and approve the blog posts. Blogs almost always need to be localized and translated in order to build emotional connections with local audiences.

Social Media

Cover all your company's social media accounts such as Twitter, Pinterest, Facebook, LinkedIn, Tumblr, and Google+. Post multiple times throughout a period of time using different copy. Define which channels, headlines, and copy work best for you. For small- and medium-sized businesses (SMBs), this is really the engine of content promotion. Pay attention to the sentiment and engagement levels from your audience.

Get fellow bloggers and internal employees to tweet, recommend, and blog about your content as another way of reaching a broader audience.

How to scale globally: Depending on company size and international presence, social media in different countries can be covered by the staff at the headquarters, if appropriate tools and process are set up. It's most effective if the social media campaigns are managed and owned by the local teams. Use local social channels with local languages in local context. Social media is more challenging to scale across countries and it's more time-consuming to do it right at a local level. *Social media is not free if you want to do it right!*

Advertising/Paid media/Outbound Marketing

Because content marketing offers educational and insightful information to an audience, you will at times want to use old-fashioned broadcast-style marketing. This still works well at the top of the purchase funnel. Search engine marketing, keyword ads, social ads, e-mail, direct mail, events, advertorials, contextual ads, native advertising, and sponsorship are all examples of paid promotions. With a relatively small budget, you can still try some pay per click (PPC) ads or sponsored tweets. With paid efforts, make sure you deliver a consistent experience from the ads to the landing sites with a crisp call-to-action.

How to scale globally: In a big enterprise, the media buy may be centralized for the local teams with a media agency of record to conduct multicountry media buys. Brief the media agency well and make sure they understand the marketing and promotional objectives so they can select the right media outlets and media placements for your content. The overall experience from the ad to the landing page where your content can be consumed or downloaded is important. Therefore, the corporate team may provide a landing page template. The local team needs to localize the template as they see fit. For smaller companies, you can purchase ad buys through an agency and work with them to determine how the media buys perform, using that feedback to optimize as you go.

E-mail

E-mail is not dead. It's an effective way to promote content and convert leads. Compelling e-mail design and catchy copywriting with a clear call-to-action still works.

How to scale globally: Corporate provides e-mail templates with a clear layout and call-to-action. Corporate may need to understand the format requirements for each country in advance. Bear in mind that e-mail may not work effectively in some countries. The local team needs to determine if this is an appropriate promotional tactic.

Events

Be ready to attend and sponsor industry events or conferences to talk about your content. As much as we love to access information online, face-to-face events are still ideal ways to promote your content. You can gauge potential customers' interest levels, answer any questions potential buyers may have, and direct them to the appropriate level of engagement. Grassroots marketing still works.

How to scale globally: Sometimes, big enterprises have their own proprietary events across regions (Intel Developer Forum, HP Discover, Microsoft's Tech Ed, etc.). If it's important to sponsor these cross-region events, corporate should negotiate multi-region sponsorships on behalf of the local teams. In general, the local team needs to determine the right local events in which to engage. Encourage your local team to attend or sponsor local events, if it makes sense.

Affiliate marketing/Partner marketing

If the content is relevant to your company's vendors, distributors, or channel partners, ask them to share your content and promote it on their Web sites or through their social media outlets. Allow your content to be co-branded with your partners' or vendors' logos. Tie your company's partner membership benefits to content promotion. For example, if your company's content is promoted, the partner receives certain points or gets products at a discount.

How to scale globally: The local teams will need to work with local vendors and distributors. Content syndication membership benefits should also apply to the local vendors and partners.

Leverage employees

Some company employees are active in social media and blog spheres. Ask internal employees to promote the content. But you should have social media guidelines and compliance policies for employees to follow when posting on behalf of your company.

How to scale globally: Headquarters can write proposed copy for various social media platforms, and employees can use social sharing tools such as GaggleAMP, Social Toaster, or Dynamic Signal to promote the content. Make the job easy for them.

Step 4: Create a Content Promotion Calendar

To create a long tail effect for your content, it's necessary to create a content promotion calendar. Determine when e-mails will be sent out, when a series of blogs will be published, when will be a good time to share an infographic, when will be convenient to review the metrics, and so on. A promotion calendar helps you track the various tactics you use and may enable you to make better use of your content by spacing and timing promotions effectively.

This promotional calendar is different than the editorial calendar that I mentioned in the "Produce" chapter. The editorial calendar helps identify the topical content that needs to be created and identify content creators; the promotional calendar focuses on the promotional timeline and channels of your targeted content. The editorial calendar focuses on what to create, who is responsible for content creation and when the content will be completed, while the promotional calendar aims at where and when to promote or syndicate your finished content.

How to scale globally: Once you determine the appropriate promotional tactics, map the tactics to a timeline. In general, the calendar needs to be driven by the local team. The local team will share the results and findings on the promotional campaigns at the corporate and local sync meetings. You will notice the promotion results differ from country to country, because promotional tactics are localized. It does not make sense to compare the results between countries. The best way is to compare results to the goals each country set for themselves and to historical content promotion programs.

> *The best way is to compare results to the goals each country set for themselves and to historical content promotion programs.*

Your Local Teams Should Lead Promotional Efforts

In general, corporate will focus on promotions in its native country. In some companies, corporate will manage the corporate-wide responsibilities and have a separate team focus on the native country's marketing activities. Corporate should offer tools to the local teams and then let them lead. Give them freedom. Sometimes, the local teams may not follow the corporate team's recommendations. As a corporate person, you need to learn to see their promotions through "local" lenses and acknowledge that sometimes what plays in Boise just doesn't work in Taipei. As a local person, you need to understand headquarters can't satisfy everyone's needs.

Promotion Across Multiple Screens

Most online content is tailored for PCs and Web pages, not for smartphones or tablets. More than 86 percent of the world's population accesses the Internet from a mobile device.[6] Make sure the landing page experience or content download is mobile friendly for iOS, Windows, and Android operating systems. Yes, it takes a lot of time, effort and budget to to get it right on multiple operating systems . Unlike PCs and web-pages, we are all still learning and exploring how to optimize our content for various mobile platforms.

Users tend to skim, rather than read, on the Web. This is even truer on mobile. It's not that people won't read on their mobile devices, it's that you have to "earn" their attention more than ever. Your main idea (primary message) needs to come through in the headline and the summary with a clear call-to-action as your secondary message. All this needs to be delivered in a way that's consumable in about ten seconds, the typical user's attention span.

How to scale globally: This is very hard to proliferate to multiple countries, given the many platforms for mobile form factors, especially in the emerging countries. Focus on one or two priority countries at first. Also, make multiscreen content promotion a standing topic to force discussion between the corporate and local teams.

Less Is More

Customers certainly have more channels than ever before to get information about your products and services. In order for your message to stick, your content or products need to be viewed at least seven times, which is an old advertising adage[7] called *the rule of seven*. In addition to consulting with friends and family, potential customers will also listen to experts and even strangers. Reviews on Yelp are a great example of checking out strangers' opinions. Marketing channels are so fragmented that marketers often feel overwhelmed.

Even though your customer may be anywhere (online or off-line), it doesn't mean that you also have to be everywhere. This is especially true for SMBs that may have little or no marketing budget. ***Focus on one or two channels with the biggest Return on Investment (ROI)***. Maybe it can be your own Web site. Make sure it's easy for your customers to find information on your Web site. For some, it can be Twitter or Facebook. Or for others, billboards, newspapers, or local TV commercials can offer the best return. Understanding your customers' journey is important. It's even more important to identify the channels that drive your business.

Promotion Increases the Chance of Serendipity

Active promotion leads to serendipitous surprises and opportunities. In the world of the Net, you won't have a full picture of how your customers and prospects find you. "Google ran a study with Shopper Sciences early in 2012, looking for 3,000 shoppers in tech, auto and finance. What [they] found were 3,000 completely different paths!"[8] Since everyone takes a different path to find us, it's important to leave bread crumbs in multiple places to increase the probability of our content being discovered and consumed. My mother-in-law, Sandra Biber Didner, author of *The Conspiracies of Dreams*, did not have a formal promotional plan to market her book. However, she notices that her book sells when she speaks at events, blogs on her Web site, or promotes her books on her Facebook page. As a blogger, I also notice that content consumption of my blog goes up on Wednesdays, the day I send a weekly e-mail to subscribers of my site. These are typical of intentional and planned promotional efforts. Some promotional tactics are routine, and we do them day in and day out.

Sometimes, it's the unplanned and carefree gesture that leads to a big surprise. I read the article in *Wired Magazine* "How One Response to a Reddit Query Became a Big-Budget Flick" which was very informative. James Erwin, a technical writer working for a financial services firm in Des Moines, had been posting on Reddit for about five months. If you are not familiar with Reddit, it is a site that considers "up" or "down"

> *Active promotion leads to serendipitous surprises and opportunities.*

votes by registered users. Popular posts rise to the top, while unpopular ones move down. You can find what people think is important, gross, funny, and so forth.

Erwin, a history buff, wrote *Encyclopedia of U.S. Military Actions*, a book of about 700,000 words. Except for libraries, no one bought his book. He was not intentionally promoting his *Encyclopedia* on Reddit when he started to publish a short 350-word post using his extensive history knowledge and references. He typed Day 1: "The 35th MEU is on the ground at Kabul, preparing to deploy to southern Afghanistan. Suddenly, it vanishes. The section of Bagram where the 35th was gathered suddenly reappears in a field outside Rome..."

People responded very positively to a series of his short posts and urged him to post more. Within two weeks of his posts, his writing caught a Hollywood producer's attention. Within two months, he had taken a leave from his job to become a full-time Hollywood screenwriter. Although it's a chance of serendipity, sharing a series of short posts on Reddit is a creative way to break through the clutter. Great content is not sufficient anymore; the placement of your content is increasingly and equally important.

> *Great content is not sufficient anymore; the placement of your content is increasingly and equally important.*

Tools Are Important

Content promotion is all about processes and tools. There is no one tool that will track every promotion channel: paid, earned, and owned. You may use a couple of content syndication tools for social media communications, yet work with a media agency for content promotion, ads, keyword buys, and other forms of media buy. Owned media syndication tends to be managed by the local or Web marketing teams with other sets of tools. Also, promotional processes and tools are closely tied with metrics. A lot of tools have metrics tracking features or dashboards associated with content syndication or publication tools. Because multiple promotional channels are used, you need to look at metrics from different sources. Some metrics will provide conflicting information and you need to make judgment calls to interpret the data. I will discuss more about measurement in the Chapter 7.

In Summary

The media landscape has changed dramatically in the past two decades with the rise of social media outlets. The cost of producing and distributing media of all kinds—words, images, video and audio streams—is so minimal that anyone can have his or her own Web site, anyone can broadcast, and anyone can be a media outlet.

Not every company needs to be a media outlet, but you need to take content where your audience goes. If your audience is very active on Twitter, you need to be on Twitter. Ultimately, select the right content for the right channels at the right time. Promotion needs to be country driven.

Content promotion requires careful planning and attention-to-detail execution. Start with your promotional objectives and make sure they tie in with your global content marketing objectives. Determine the right budget to support your efforts. Prioritize promotional channels with relevant content with catchy copy and headlines. Create a schedule to bring it to life. Make sure if a tree falls in a forest, everyone is around to hear about it.

For Entrepreneurs and Small Businesses Owners

▶ Promotion is harder than creating content. With limited budget, it may be best to focus on social media.

▶ Create different copy and formats for different social channels. One size does not fit all.

▶ Try limited ad buys or PPC buys to compare paid versus organic results. Analyze the results to determine how to optimize for future content promotion.

For Enterprise Marketing Managers

▶ If budget allows, create an integrated promotion for both inbound and outbound marketing campaigns.

▶ For content promotion, corporate provides tools and a list of content, while the local teams select the content to localize and own the overall promotional plan.

▶ Tailor different copy and different formats for different marketing channels. Deliver a consistent experience from ads to the landing page. Make it easy for your audience to convert.

For Agencies and Marketing Consultants

▶ Depending on the engagement scope with your clients, understand your client's promotional plans.

▶ Help them create different copy and formats for different promotion channels.

▶ Be proactive and help them identify tools that will make promotion or content syndication easy.

CASE STUDY

Content Fuels DocuSign's Demand Generation

Have you ever electronically and digitally signed a document? If yes, then it's very likely you used a tool provided by DocuSign. This company provides electronic signature technology and digital transaction management services for facilitating electronic exchanges of legally binding contracts and signed documents. Their products support 44 languages and are used in over 188 countries.[9] The marketing team targets anyone who is over the age of 18 with an e-mail address that has the legal right to sign a document. Realtors can use DocuSign's tools to ask clients to sign documents electronically. University administrators can ask students to sign financial aid agreements. Human Resources managers can ask new employees to sign non-disclosure agreements. Hospital receptionists can ask patient to sign privacy waivers. Literally, any profession can be its potential customers. With that in mind, DocuSign projects the number of total potential customers is over a billion people. It's not a surprise that it has identified 20 global personas.

Content is the most effective way to educate their targeted personas on how easy and convenient it is to use DocuSign to send and sign documents anytime, anywhere on any screen. According to Meagen Eisenberg, VP of Demand Generation, content also plays an important role for lead generation and nurturing. When she joined DocuSign back in 2011, Eisenberg conducted a content audit and created a massive spreadsheet to understand the existing content landscape for key personas. With her team as part of the central marketing group, she mapped existing content to the buyers' journey and identified missing content at different stages. To fill that gap, she worked with the team to build a roadmap of the necessary content. With limited resources and budget, it would be tough to focus on all 20 personas simultaneously, so they prioritized three key personas to drive demand: Sales, Human Resources, and

Procurement. She also worked closely with her sales team and created unique nurture programs for different buying stages with specific content. She even wrote a dozen content items by herself. Using that content as a base, she hired and trained content creators to tailor content for different personas as well as outside domain experts to write whitepapers. The team slowly extended core programs to the other personas. Some of the common types of content for nurturing programs are case studies, webinars, customer quotes, demos, trials and whitepapers.

Over a two-year span, the team built over 80 nurture programs with very targeted lead lists using a marketing automation tool—Eloqua. Through segmentation and automation, these programs helped drive more leads through the sales funnel at a faster rate. Within three months of the first dozen nurture programs going live, leads doubled for the corporate business and the following quarter after two dozen programs went live, it tripled.

The DocuSign content efforts have multiple uses within the company extending from customer support to the sales teams. Since DocuSign is embedded into software such as Salesforce.com, Microsoft 365, Box, Comcast, NetSuite, FoxIt, etc., the content is also incorporated into partner marketplaces and onboarding. In addition, the same marketing automation tool is deployed worldwide and the nurture programs extend to other regions around the world. Their European region localized several of the nurture programs to drive regional demand generation efforts. The local team will determine the localization and translation required.

When Meagen joined DocuSign in 2011, it was roughly a 150-person company. Now, it has grown to over 850 on a trajectory to hit 1,300—all in less than three years. Like the company, content planning and creation efforts are also going through a growth phase. The fun is just starting!

CASE STUDY

Diary of a Content Pimp 3: The Promotion Plan Without Budget

(Originally published on Velocity blog on July 2nd, 2012)

Doug Kessler, Creative Director at Velocity in the United Kingdom, wrote a fun blog about how to promote its hero content, "The Content Marketing Strategy Checklist." It's a fun read. Because the team has no promotional budget, they offer their blood, toil, tears, and sweat. OK, mostly, Kessler and his team offer their time and human resources to create and implement a detailed promotional plan. This blog post provides some recommendations to SMBs on how to promote their content. Here is the original blog post.

We despair when we see business-to-business (B2B) brands producing terrific content, then just sticking it on their virtual shelf and maybe sending out the odd tweet. What a waste.

We worked too hard on The Content Marketing Strategy Checklist to just leave its distribution to chance. So we made a plan.

Our Marketing Plan

A content promotion plan can be a detailed document full of media-speak like reach, frequency, impressions, CPM, CPC, and . . . budget.

Ours is far simpler, largely because we *have* no budget. It's kind of liberating in the same way that an acute shortage of bells is liberating to a Morris dancer.

Why aren't we spending big behind the Checklist? Because we feel we can hit our targets by investing a bit of time instead of a lot of money. We might do the occasional experiment with pay-per-click ads or web banners but they'll be just that: experiments.

When you don't have any money to spend, it's even more important to have at least a cursory plan. Here is our plan:

The Five Pillars of Content Promotion

Almost every content promotion plan should have at least a token bit of these five tactics:

Search

To make sure your content get discovered, it's best to think about your key phrases before you start. Otherwise you end up with clunky titles like The Content Marketing Strategy Checklist. (See Diary of a Content Pimp 1: the kickoff to see why we called it that.)

The search part of our promotion plan is basically about getting the key phrases right (Content Marketing Strategy) and making sure we do all the hygiene things Google likes (titles, tags, URLs, blah, blah, blah). We then track how we're doing and panic accordingly.

(As I write this, the Checklist landing page listing is towards the bottom of page 1 of the U.K. Google results for "Content Marketing Strategy." Not bad from a standing start but not where we want to be.)

Under Search, we might also do some PPC experiments but only because it's fun. Call us old-fashioned but paying ten quid per conversion just doesn't feel like value in our world.

Social

For cheapskates of our ilk, this is really the engine of content promotion. So we're blogging about the Checklist (like . . . now) and tweeting the hell out of it and posting in LinkedIn groups and making cute little pins on Pinterest.

We've also given the bloggers we respect most a sneak preview of the Checklist. They gave us fantastic feedback and suggestions for improvements. And they've been really wonderful advocates out there in social-land. (A single tweet from a David Meerman Scott, Michael Brenner, Joe Pulizzi, Ashley Friedlein or Maria Pergolino is worth *hundreds* of tweets from that manic "personal branding" coach on crack.)

Outbound

Outbound marketing is way out of fashion but it's about to make a comeback. Only this time, instead of pushing products into people's faces, we'll be pushing content at them.

That may disappoint those marketers who thought "old-school, interruption-based, broadcast-style" marketing was dead. It's not. We're marketers and it's our job to interrupt people (intelligently) and to broadcast our stories (in relevant channels).

The good news: a content offer will almost always out-perform a product offer—especially at the top of the funnel, where the wild prospects hang out.

Our outbound marketing for the Checklist consists of e-mail. Because we put some of our content behind web forms ("Boo!", "Hiss!" Get over it.), we've built a pretty good list of B2B marketers who are interested in content marketing.

We're segmenting that list and using different creative concepts and visuals to lure these fine folks back for the Checklist.

Any other outbound? We may test a few PPC ads, sponsored tweets (if we can buy one from a friend) or banner ads. I'd love to test retargeting but I think our budget is too low (and it does tend to creep me out).

Lead Nurturing

You can't just fling stuff at people, wait a while, then fling some more. We're using Neil's Magic Marketo Machine to manage all of the above efforts, laying down content stepping stones all the way to our virtual door. (We'll report on these experiments in future Pimp Diary posts.)

What's cool is that you can see things like, "Bob Bonobo opened the e-mail, downloaded the Checklist, then visited eight more pages on our site, got the Content Marketing Workbook and signed up for our newsletter." If Mr. Bonobo also happens to be the CMO of Adobe, the old Pavlov salivation kicks in and Stan starts baying at the moon. Video to follow.

Content Atomization

One big chunky piece of content (like the Checklist) is a really powerful asset. But spinning it out in to 15-20 more pieces makes it rocket fuel.

How will we atomize the Content Marketing Strategy Checklist?

- ▶ **Blog posts** – where we'll take one topic from the Checklist and drill down.

- ▶ **Diary of a content pimp** – a special blog series that … oh, you know this already.

- ▶ **Guest blogging** – on great sites like Econsultancy and the Content Marketing Institute.

- ▶ **A slideshare sample** – we posted the first ten pages of the Checklist on Slideshare as a sample, with a big, crass CTA as page 11. Is it working? We'll let you know. (93 views in first eight days – traffic and conversion data to follow.)

- ▶ **Infographics** – watch this space (if we didn't crank out at least one infographic around this we'd be in breach of about 20 B2B statutes).

- ▶ **Prezis** – we like Prezi for B2B content marketing.

- ▶ **Shorter papers** – which we'll offer without a web form ("Hurrah!" Sheesh.).

- ▶ **Video** – we aim to do at least one "chalk talk" on Checklist topics. Maybe more.

- ▶ **Webinars** – we're really bad at doing these for ourselves and need to get better.

- ▶ **Conference sessions** – have passport, will speak (banjo optional)

You get the idea. Content Atomization takes your original content into new places where different communities hang out. Then, ideally, tractor-beams the best prospects back to the mother ship for anal probing. (Or whatever nurturing process you favour.)

Content Atomization Tip: you can't just cut and paste into new media; you've got to add value and spin the content for each channel and audience. (Well, the Slideshare sample was a cut and paste...)

Our First Ten Weeks: A Content Promotion Calendar

We're going to pace ourselves here. Content marketing is an Olympic Triathlon, not a three-legged sack race.

Some of the things in our plan won't be happening in the first months. Others will. It really helps to scribble up a content promotion calendar—everyone does editorial calendars but we don't see enough of these. Here's our content promotion calendar for weeks 1-10:

First Ten Weeks		21/6	25/6	2/6	9/7	16/7	23/7	30/7	6/8	13/8
	1	2	3	4	5	6	7	8	9	10
Pre-share	X									
Launch		X								
E-mail		X	X		X			X		
Blog 1/wk		X	X	X	X	X	X	X	X	X
Guest				X			X			X
Social		X	X	X	X	X	X	X	X	X
Infographic							X			
Slideshare			X							
KPI Check		X	X	X	X	X	X	X	X	X

Kessler graciously shared the promotional results with me. They met some goals and missed some. Overall, they consider this content delivered the results they were looking for. Well-done, Doug!

Content Marketing Strategy Checklist

Goal	After 6 months (19/6/12–18/12/12)	All time results (19/6/12–16/4/14)	Source
Conversions			
1500 downloads	2,156	10,039	Google Analytics
10% goal conversion rate (checklist downloads)	7.40%	5.40%	Google Analytics
47% funnel conversion rate	42%	72%	Google Analytics
Engagement			
2.5+ Average Page depth from landing page entrances (all sources)	2.17	1.68	Google Analytics
<50% bounce rate from landing page entrances (all sources)	53.40%	48.50%	Google Analytics
<25% bounce rate from landing page entrances (e-mail)	35.70%	35.10%	Google Analytics
SEO			
500 new entrances from non-branded traffic	589	4,128	Google Analytics
25 backlinks (referring domains)	20	74	MajesticSEO
30 comments on landing page	59	100	WordPress

Other

Goal	After 6 months (19/6/12–18/12/12)	All time results (19/6/12–16/4/14)	Source
Business goals			
10 new meetings (from all content library)	9	13–15	Management
20% new bizz conversion rate (from all content library)	n/a	n/a	Management
Converstions			
700 extra downloads of other gated content	1,519	8,636	Google Analytics
500 other converstions	89 newsletter sign ups	1,422 newsletter sign ups	Google Analytics
SEO			
Rank #2 (UK) from [B2B Content Marketing]	n/a	#1	Google
Rank #4 (USA) from [B2B Content Marketing]	n/a	#8	Google
Social			
800 Twitter shares (from campaign landers)	n/a	720	Sharecount
400 LinkedIn shares (from campaign landers)	n/a	779	Sharecount
200 Facebook shares (from campaign landers)	n/a	291	Sharecount
100 Printerest shares (from campaign landers)	n/a	0	Sharecount

CHAPTER SEVEN

The Fourth P of the Global Content Marketing Cycle: Perfect

Definition of Perfect

Perfect (pronounced per-fekt) is to continuously optimize and measure the impact of content marketing as part of an ongoing feedback loop. Define goals and use tools and processes to maximize the effectiveness of content production and content syndication. To improve the previous 3 P's: Plan, Produce, and Promote.

> *"Don't measure what you can. Measure what you should."*
>
> **—PHILIP SHELDRAKE**[1]

So, What Should We Measure Anyway?

Philip Sheldrake's quote makes me ponder, "For content marketing, what should we measure anyway?" On the surface, it seems like an easy question to answer. My initial instinct:

"Well, measure content against our business and marketing objectives." When I peel one layer deeper, I realize that it's not that easy. How do we measure "content" against business or marketing objectives? Historically in most organizations, there is no department or center of excellence called *content*.

Content tends to reside within each marketing function or within business units. Content is decentralized and is everywhere. In addition, content tends to be viewed as an enabler, not an outcome. It's easy to measure an outcome and much harder to measure an "enabler." Let's take events as an example: Content such as training classes and keynotes is part of a company's customer event. We measure the event in terms of number of attendees, number of mentions in press clips, number of mentions in social media, number of leads entered into Customer Relationship Management (CRM), yet the content is typically measured by surveys asking attendees to evaluate the training sessions and keynotes. The good survey results, however, do not usually tie back to the business or marketing objectives beyond the conference itself, even though training sessions and keynotes are critical mediums to promote the company's messages.

> Content tends to be viewed as an enabler, not an outcome. It's easy to measure an outcome and much harder to measure an "enabler."

Here is another example: content as communications materials on web landing pages. We focus on time spent, content downloads, and conversion rate as part of the landing page metrics, but there is no measurement of content in the landing page metrics. With the rise of self-broadcasting such as YouTube, podcasts, and other channels, content can now be both an enabler **and** an outcome. By featuring content as a webinar or webcast, potential leads can be generated from the attendees. Some companies even charge for webinars or podcasts. Suddenly, content can generate revenue for a company. However, the metrics focus solely on the number of registrants for the webinar. The webinar itself tends to be classified as an element of demand generation or online marketing programs rather than as a stand-alone content element.

Here are several reasons why content marketing is in the backseat of marketing:

► No "content marketing" group or center of excellence exists. Most companies have events marketing, advertising, social media, direct marketing, online marketing, demand generation, creative services, sales operations, or even partner marketing. Content tends to reside within each department.

► Content is an enabler, not an outcome. Content is in everything. It's like air, which is everywhere. How do you measure the impact of air (except when it's polluted or missing)?

► Because content is embedded in every department, it's hard to hold one department or one person accountable.

► Senior management doesn't understand the benefits and revenue impact of content marketing and sees only costs associated with it. However, content has the potential to become a revenue-generating machine.

► Content creation is decentralized and/or outsourced; there is no internal champion or a spokesperson.

If you have created a global content plan and aligned the plan with key stakeholders, your company is ahead of the curve. If you are struggling to push a content plan through and still trying to get key stakeholders' buy-in, you are not alone. Do the best you can. Content marketing education is not a sprint; it's an Ironman Triathlon.

> *Content marketing education is not a sprint; it's an Ironman Triathlon.*

Now back to what we should measure.

Let's Face It: Measuring Content Is Hard!

Content, design, and experience have something in common. All of them are hard to translate into sales figures, even though we all know that they're incredibly important.

Without content, there is no way to guide our audience to and within our Web sites. Without content, we have nothing to use to engage our audience. Without content, it's hard to communicate with our audience about our products and our brand. Content plays a vital role and it's an integral part of marketing communications. It's the unsung hero, yet it rarely gets a byline or any praise. If content wants to have a seat at a management table, then content's value needs to be quantified.

As part of the global content plan discussed in Chapter 4, we stressed the importance of aligning key success metrics with business and marketing objectives. Say, the sales objective is to increase sales from $10 million to $20 million in the healthcare segment in the United States and China. Some examples of marketing objectives could be:

▶ Establish your company's products as a preferred choice by doctors and hospital administrators.

▶ Deliver 5,000 leads per quarter from inbound traffic through progressive nurturing using content marketing.

▶ Enable sales team wins by delivering sales training and sales enablement content.

The measurements should align with the examples of marketing objectives above:

▶ Brand preference

▶ Lead generation

▶ Sales enablement

The challenge is not how to measure brand preference, lead generation, and sales enablement. We all know how to do that. The challenge is how to measure the effectiveness and contribution of content in the context of brand preference, lead generation, and sales enablement.

It's important to understand what you create content for and understand how that content relates, directly or indirectly, to your marketing objectives.

Here is another challenge. Some types of content we create or share won't have a direct tie to sales. It doesn't mean that the value of that content piece is diminished. It only means that the content serves different objectives such as building awareness, focusing press coverage pickup, or positioning the company as a thought leader. Here is the takeaway from this chapter: It's important to understand what you create content for and understand how that content relates, directly or indirectly, to your marketing objectives. Although aligning content metrics with business objectives is important and mandatory, we should not stop there. There are other measurements that we should consider tracking for the impact of content beyond business-oriented key success metrics.

I Have Been Looking for the Wrong Metrics All Along

As a content creator, I often ask who are the viewers and how many downloads of the content I created. For the content we create or distribute, we love to know the total numbers of views or downloads from all the syndication channels. Having a big download number seems to be a good way to validate our work. Here is the challenge: The content itself may reside on the company's Web site, but the same piece of content has also been distributed on YouTube, iTunes, and other social media sites. It can also be presented as part of paid advertising as an advertorial, native advertising, or a customized promotional program. We use different tools to measure paid, earned, and owned media. *It's almost impossible to consolidate all the media measurements to find that absolute and total number of views and downloads for an individual piece of content.* So, no matter what we do, the numbers we collect are never complete. At the same time, that download or number of views is just a figure at a given time. In the Chapter 6 case study, the Promotional Plan without Budget, Doug Kessler shared the metric results six months after the launch of the flagship content and results up to April, 2014. Because content can be evergreen, the number will never stay the same.

Here is the thing: the number by itself really doesn't mean much. Even if you have a goal, it still really doesn't mean much. *That number does not really tell me if the content creates any business impact.* Here are some good examples of impact: If that content had over 50,000 views, and it was picked up by the press, and created free media coverage for our company, that's impact. If less than 100 people viewed that content, but one of them is the CEO of a company we have been targeting for six months, that piece of intelligence is important for our sales team so they can follow up and start a conversation with that company. That's impact. Thus, asking for the total viewership of that content is not the right question to ask to understand the business impact. I have been asking the wrong questions all along.

I should have asked questions differently:

▶ What objectives are we trying to accomplish? (This is important, but tends to be ignored.)

▶ How is the content being used?

▶ In what context is the content being used?

▶ How does the content contribute to different metrics in paid, owned, and earned media?

> Content can't be measured alone. It needs to be measured as a function of something.

Again, content can't be measured alone. It needs to be measured as a function of something. If you focus on awareness as an objective, the content you create is intended to drive interest in your products and brands. One possible awareness tactic is to use paid media to promote your company and content. If your objective is solely to drive leads or drive sales on your e-commerce site, you may focus on leveraging paid and social media to drive traffic to your site and beef up the amount of original content on your sites with compelling offers to entice potential customers to opt-in or purchase. The true value of content in this objective is to drive conversions, not necessarily the number of likes or shares.

Steve Radick, VP of Public Relations (PR) at Cramer-Krasselt, posted a blog on Ragan's PR Daily[2]: "If your goal is to increase e-commerce sales, show how much traffic is coming in through your social channels. If your goal is to improve your brand's online reputation, point to the quality of the search results. If your goal is to increase awareness, point to the total number of mentions across all media channels..."

His post echoes my point of view of measuring the "impact" of content in relationship to business and marketing objectives. Steve points out that it's vital to quantify social media efforts contributing to your company's business goals. Rather than measuring "likes," "numbers of followers," "shares" and more, focus on how social media facilitates and helps achieving your business goals. *Always come back to your objectives to determine the measurements you should track.*

Think Differently About Content Measurements

I often feel content is like a piece of furniture. A sofa is a sofa. The quality and the style of the sofa are important. The quality and beauty of the sofa can only be highlighted nicely when it's placed properly in a nicely designed living room and is matched with the right decor and colors. A piece of content is a piece of content. It's hard to measure content alone! So how should we measure content? *The usefulness of content can only be quantified when external customers see it and then take some sort of action, or internal stakeholders use it.* I'd define the value of content like this:

$$\textit{Value of Content = F (Content Usage to Deliver Organizational Impact)}$$

The benefit of a piece of content can only be realized when it's used or placed properly to bring a return to an organization (see Figure 7.01). The impact can be tangible, solid, and

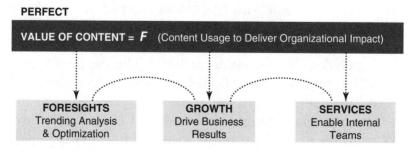

PERFECT

VALUE OF CONTENT = *F* (Content Usage to Deliver Organizational Impact)

| FORESIGHTS | GROWTH | SERVICES |
| Trending Analysis & Optimization | Drive Business Results | Enable Internal Teams |

FIGURE 7.01 Measure the Impact of Content

quantifiable, such as generating new prospects, retaining customers for sell-up, or enabling sales teams. The impact can also be intangible, soft, and qualitative such as comments, shares, and anecdotes. You need to capture both tangible and intangible impacts. At the same time, you need to educate internal stakeholders and management on the added value of content and help them see content through different lenses. The value of content as a function of delivering organizational impact can be categorized into three groups:

- ▶ F (Growth): Drive Business Results
- ▶ F (Foresight): Share Trending Insights and Optimize Content
- ▶ F (Services): Enable Internal Groups to Use Content More Effectively

Growth: Measurements that inform us *"how we did."* Absolute values by themselves have no meaning. We need a baseline and/or a goal to put numbers into context. This goal can be an industry benchmark, a target based on past history, or a target set by management. Measurement is only meaningful when it's related to or compared with something. When we report to senior management, we tend to report on how we did against goals.

> *Foresights: Measurements that guide "how we should improve."*

Foresights: Measurements that guide *"how we should improve."* It can be a continuous and frequent effort of optimizing the placement and quality of content. It can also use predictive analytics of Big Data[3] to find relationships in data not readily apparent with traditional analysis. Although we are trying to optimize for the future, information is gleaned from past trends and patterns, whether the analysis is done by humans or machines. This can be as simple as A/B testing[4] or as complicated as Big Data descriptive and predictive analysis.

Other tactical questions that should be answered are: When is the optimal day of the week and time of day to post your content? Which headline works better?

Some questions require more extensive data analysis: How effective are our social media programs? Can we predict the next content piece that our target customers will consume? The analysis and testing should give us some clues about what we should do next, but we need to continually evaluate and adjust our course as we go.

Services: This measurement answers the question, ***"What has content done for our organization lately?"*** This needs to be a deliberate effort, which can be very hard to automate. You need to proactively reach out to other business units to document the work you do for them and how your content is being used for internal communications or executive keynotes and more. To showcase the holistic impact of content, the soft and intangible side of content can't be ignored.

> *Services: This measurement answers the question, "What has content done for our organization lately?"*

Educate Your Management About the Impact of Content

During the regular metrics report to senior management, it's typical to share measurements that are tied to business results. That's what everyone cares about. It's also important to share lessons learned and the next steps with other departments and internal customers so they understand what you will be doing to help the organization as a whole. ***Have one slide to share two or three things you will do to improve content and content marketing.*** Focus on high-level actions, not too much working detail. What to share also depends on what your management is interested in knowing. By all means, this is not a complete list, but here are some recommendations to consider what to share, in addition to regular metrics to report:

- ▶ Top 3–5 content pieces that drove the most leads and why.
- ▶ Which specific channel drives more traffic to the landing page other than tactics? You may allocate some dollars to test if incremental leads can be generated before it hits the diminishing rate of return.

- ▶ A list of content added to the sales training portal as part of a sales training kit.
- ▶ Interesting customer feedback and comments about the company and products after consuming the content you syndicate.

Understand what content-related information your management is interested in and why. Fully realize the value of content and think holistically on how content helps the company, not just for business and marketing objectives.

Measuring Content by Its Impact

It still makes sense that the basic measurements of content are numbers of views, clicks, downloads, shares, and forwards. These are measurements we can easily track and have in place to determine tactical effectiveness of some types of campaigns.

At a strategic level, we should track how content delivers impact to organizations. Examples of standard impact metrics are conversions, leads, sales opportunities or sales volume, and PR buzz.

To understand the impact of content, the infrastructure or processes need to be connected from the top of the purchase funnel all the way to closed sales. In order to accomplish this tracking, you may need to use marketing automation tools and integrate them with your other company systems. For instance, if a CTO of a targeted account downloads a piece of content, you won't know this person's relationship with your company unless that lead information is reconciled with your CRM. It's very difficult to find out if the press picks up your content unless you use Google Alerts or a social listening tool. Without tools such as these, it's almost impossible to track the impact of content. You would need to pull data from different resources, which is very difficult and time-consuming. *Processes and tools are as important as strategies and plans, but they tend to be overlooked by marketing and treated as an afterthought.*

Measurement Category	Characters of Measurements	Measured as Function of	Examples of Metrics Related to Content
F (Growth): Drive Business Results	How did we do?	Customer acquisition Customer retention, up-sell, cross-sell	The leads/conversions need to be triangulated with CRM, marketing automation tools, and other tools to show impact on volume, sales, and costs. Social listening and other tools are needed.
		Customer education and awareness	▲ Downloads of gated content, cost per download, projected sales volume
			▲ Content leads to newsletter subscription, cost per subscription
		Sales enablement and training	▲ Content leads to click on buy now button, cost per click, sales volume
			▲ Content leads to 1-800 toll free numbers, cost per call, sales volume
			▲ Content leads to registration of webinars or sponsored events, cost per registration, sales volume
			▲ Conversions on landing pages by content consumption
			▲ Analyze behavior or sales performance changes by comparing sales team who consumed content versus who didn't
F (Foresights): Share Trending Insights and Optimize Content	How should we improve for the future?	Content optimization to improve growth and sales Big Data predictive or prescriptive analytics	▲ Metrics depend on what needs to be optimized. ▲ Metrics depend on what issues need to be resolved using Big Data.

(Continued)

Measurement Category	Characters of Measurements	Measured as Function of	Examples of Metrics Related to Content
F (Services): Enable Internal Groups to Use Content More Effectively	What has content done for our organization lately?	Content's usage for internal communications Customer services department Projects taken to support other divisions Content for executive communications	▲ Number of content pieces used for internal communications ▲ Content used to train customer service reps ▲ Content forwarded to customer as part of customer services engagements ▲ Number of content consulting projects to support other divisions ▲ Number of content pieces used for keynote and executive presentations

Driving Business Results

Measure Content as Customer Acquisition and Retention

This is the most common and understandable measurement for content marketing and is easy to grasp for management and the sales team. The main benefit of content is to help the company acquire, nurture, and convert leads. In order to show the impact of content, the first step is to have a holistic view of how your company's acquisition, nurturing, and conversion processes are tracked across multiple channels. By understanding the process, you know what content is used, where it is placed, and how content performs. It helps you tell a more complete story about how content delivers an impact to customer acquisition and retention.

In general, new customers come from trade shows and/or industry events, e-mail campaigns, display ads, retargeting, registration through gated content, newsletter subscriptions, downloads from landing pages, media promotions, and more. Draw a process flow chart to understand how customers are acquired by various marketing efforts in your company. You can see how each department uses content. Document the processes and tools on the flow chart. You can also correlate data across different campaigns and marketing channels to determine which channels work better. If the processes and tools are not integrated, this flow chart will help you to understand where the tools are missing. Identify these gaps to discuss further with key stakeholders.

Some examples of content specific impact to drive leads:

- ▶ Opt-ins to download gated content
- ▶ Content leads to newsletter subscription
- ▶ Content leads to click on "buy now" button
- ▶ Content leads to 1-800 toll free numbers
- ▶ Content leads to registration for webinars or sponsored events

It's easy to capture the total number of newsletter subscriptions, but it may take effort to sift through the details to further quantify the impact of content. It's OK to estimate a content contribution percentage based on your analysis, but make sure that the relevant stakeholders support your assumptions and conclusions.

How to scale globally: Customer acquisition goals need to be set at a country level. Each country's acquisition efforts and channels may be managed differently. Some tools are deployed from the corporate level while some tools are homegrown or purchased at the country or regional level. It does not mean that the content requirements will be completely different. As long as countries follow the same marketing objectives and target the same audience, there is content that should apply across different geographies. However, some content will need to be localized or created locally as discussed in Chapter 5. How content performs to support customer acquisition and retention at the geographical and national level should be a standing topic during recurring headquarters and local sync meetings.

Measure Content as Customer Education and Awareness

Not all the content you create will drive direct sales engagements. Some content you create is to educate customers or build awareness about specific fields, specific challenges, or even specific usages, which may not directly relate to your products or services. Yet, providing such types of content has the long-term benefit of building relationships with your customers or positioning your company as a thought leader. In general, it's very challenging to measure the business results of education or awareness-oriented content, unless it's tied with a call-to-action or offering that you can track. Because it's so hard to track the results of these types of content, some companies try to discreetly place a company logo, contact information, calls to action, or offers into the flow or layout of content. By doing so, they may be able to track the performance of specific content if the customers respond to the embedded offers.

> *Not all the content you create will drive direct sales engagements.*

In general, it's hard to measure the direct impact of customer education and awareness on business goals, yet it's a critical part of content marketing. However, if the call to action and offer response from educational and awareness content is very low, you can't justify the investment in content creation. There are times when you have a gut feeling that creating and placing certain content is the right thing to do but, without hard data to back up your conviction, you may be unable to convince management to allocate budget. Management is often interested in looking at potential investments purely from the perspective of hard numbers and may question any soft or indirect returns you specify. Here are some recommendations to help you convince management to continue to support your content marketing efforts:

▶ Defense: Show budget breakdown between sales-driven and education-driven content. Communicate that educational and awareness content as the overall percentages of content budget is not big.

▶ Offense: Show how competitors effectively use educational and awareness content to showcase their thought leadership and expertise.

▶ Extreme offense: Completely stop creating educational and awareness-related content and compare the sales before and after the decisions to prove if educational and awareness makes sense for your company. For long purchase cycles, this may take three to nine months to show the differences.

How to scale globally: If your products are homogenous, it's easy to scale educational and awareness content. When you create content, focus on common pain points, challenges, and desires, or your company's unique expertise. The challenge is that different countries may use different marketing channels to educate their target audience. Depending on what channel(s) they choose, different formats of content and channels may be required, which in turn may force a change in appropriate measurements. Due to budget and resource constraints, some geographies may choose to focus only on lead generation which directly ties with sales efforts.

Measure Content as a Function of Sales Enablement

Depending on the company and industry, the sales enablement function can reside within the sales team, sales operations, or marketing. On the surface, it may seem as if there is no relationship between sales enablement and content marketing. A relationship can and should exist, especially when the sales enablement team can leverage content created by the content marketing team or the content producers can take the technical sales training and turn it into more educational materials for their target audience. I shared how we can leverage sales enablement content as part of global content planning in Chapter 5.

The benefit of sales enablement is to prepare the sales team well, so they can solely focus on what they do well—SELL. The sales enablement or the sales operations team usually has a service level agreement (SLA) with the sales team. The SLA should form the basis for the success metrics measurement for the efforts of the sales enablement team on behalf of the sales group. Typical sales enablement metrics tend to measure sales training and training materials consumption.

Joellen Sorenson Director of Solutions Marketing at the SAVO Group, wrote a great blog post, "Accountable Sales Enablement," to measure the impact of sales enablement efforts. She stresses that we should measure sales enablement by both "consumption and impact."[5] She defined "impact" as a way to foster positive changes in field behavior and improvements in sales performance. She suggested reconciling content consumption data with sales performance data in CRM. Compare sales representatives who consume content and training against the ones who don't. Analyze the data to understand if content consumption drives positive sales behavior changes and improves sales performance.

Examples of content consumption related metrics as a function of sales enablement:

- ▶ Content usage
  - ▶ Number of content downloads
  - ▶ Number of new hires trained through sales onboarding program

> ▶ Numbers of dedicated collaterals and messages for targeted audience, territories, and vertical segments
> ▶ Number of sales representatives receiving sales kits and new product training prior to product launches

▶ Content and expert access improvement

> ▶ Measurement for correlation data between an increase in sales activity and decreased time logged into the sales library site or the sales enablement portal
> ▶ Measurement for quick access to subject matter experts to assist sales

▶ Examples of impact of sales behavior and sales performance

> ▶ Compare if the reps that attended a cross-selling training display get better results than the ones who didn't attend.
> ▶ Compare if the new hires who were involved in onboarding ramped quicker than their predecessors who didn't attend onboarding.

In general, sales enablement metrics usually are not tracked as part of global content marketing measurements. However, if you are involved in sales enablement content creation or the sales enablement team uses your materials as part of sales training kits or onboarding, you need to understand their metrics. You should not take all the credit for content consumption, but you need to articulate how your content contributes to content consumption or impacts sales enablement measurements.

How to scale globally: English as a universal language usually works well across multiple countries. If your company's official language is not English and you are rapidly expanding to other regions, it makes sense to have sales training in both the native language and English. The sales enablement team is most likely based at headquarters, so you may need to create sales collaterals in both the native language and English to train sales teams in other regions and countries. Sales enablement metrics should be tracked at a country level then rolled up to headquarters. The collateral used by the sales team for their customers may need to be localized and translated.

Measure Content Optimization
to Improve Growth and Sales

In the context of this book, there are two primary ways to improve content in order to drive a company's growth:

▶ The quality of content

▶ The placement of content

Improving the quality of content means to improve topics, headlines, copy, writing, formats, storytelling, editing, and search engine optimization (SEO). It's pretty much anything we can do to make the content itself better, based on quantifiable data and personal judgments. To improve the placement of content is to promote content in ideal locations where your target audience will easily encounter it. These two elements can directly and indirectly influence sales leads, which potentially impacts sales. The process of improving the quality and placement of content is called *content optimization*.

> *Improving the quality of content means to improve topics, headlines, copy, writing, formats, storytelling, editing, and search engine optimization (SEO).*

Some companies test content before a broad rollout. This is usually true for media companies such as Upworthy and Mashable. Try to test various headlines for the same content with a small percentage of the audience in real time. Optimizing and capturing the test results before you distribute the content widely is the best practice for content marketers. By doing so, your content will hopefully perform better, which directly impacts the business results.

In general, most content optimization metrics are tedious and only matter to content creators and marketing managers who are engaged in the respective marketing activities. This is not typically something that management cares to know. However, if you or your agency can summarize the results succinctly and quantify some of the progress with specific numbers related to sales, this may have a positive impact on management's perception of the content marketing efforts. It's important to communicate with management how you are constantly challenging the status quo by monitoring content closely in an effort to optimize it to improve sales performance.

For example, you create two different videos telling the same story: one video showcases several customers describing your new products and their experience; the other video is a fun animation describing your new products and features. The objective is to communicate the features and benefits of the new products using the same content format which is video, yet the storytelling approach is different. Both are uploaded to YouTube and promoted the same amount of frequency and time through social media channels. If the testimonial video drives more leads to the landing page, you may share that insight and ask the sales team to convince more customers to participate. If the animation performs better, you can communicate how you would put more promotion behind that type of content as it seems to be driving more leads. You can also choose to make a recommendation of scaling back on customer testimonials. That recommendation may not be the politically correct thing to do, yet solid data may persuade the sales team and management of your suggested approach. A compromise to make the scaling back on customer testimonials more palatable might be to find different uses for that content, such as incorporating it into a senior manager's keynote, external presentation, or as a video that runs on flat panels in booths at events.

Insights to optimize the quality of content:

▶ Storytelling and creative approach: Because content may be aimed at different objectives, make sure you compare content with similar objectives.

▶ Length of content: Run testing to determine the optimal length for different formats of content.

▶ Headlines, copy: Write multiple versions of headlines and copy and conduct A/B testing with small subsets of your audience.

▶ Format selection: Sometimes, stories implicitly determine an appropriate format based on the content itself. Other times you will need to choose a format and then determine the storytelling or your creative approach.

▶ SEO: Optimize your content with key words, but don't force it.

Insights to optimize the placement of content:

▶ Placement on the landing page: Our eyes gravitate to a certain area of landing pages or mobile sites. In business, we say: "Location, location, location." Location of your content has an impact on the consumption. Some companies have human factors or user design experts who can help optimize your layout.

▶ Placement on various media properties or social media sites: This should be tested to determine the effectiveness of various media outlets for specific types of content.

▶ Frequency and timing of placement: Run testing to determine how many times the content should be promoted and the timing of placement.

▶ Budget allocation between various paid and organic sites: Optimize the budget allocation among various sites to maximize the impact.

Metrics for the quality and placement of content vary depending on what you want to optimize. Ultimately, the goals need to tie your content back to achieving your business and marketing objectives more effectively.

How to scale globally: Optimization needs to be driven at the country level. This is not a task for which headquarters should take the lead. What headquarters can do is to facilitate the knowledge exchange between geographies and countries during the regularly scheduled synch meetings with the geographies. The headquarters may be able to provide recommendations on tools and establish processes and templates, but ultimately, the local teams need to commit to use the tools, processes and templates.

Measure Content as Big Data Analysis

Everything we do online is somehow captured by someone or some enterprise.

Our purchasing and content consumption behavior has been revolutionized by mobile devices, the cloud, social media, and search. Everything we do online is somehow captured by someone or some enterprise.

Our daily searches are captured by search engine companies while our online purchase transactions are captured by e-commerce sites. Our posts on social media platforms are no exception. In reality, the tasks we perform off-line are also tracked. Just driving to work generates data in newer cars as they now record engine functions and the next time you have the car serviced, this data gets uploaded and analyzed to identify any issues with the car.[6]

According to IBM's 2014 Global CMO study, we create 2.5 quintillion (10^{18}) bytes of data every day.[7] There are 30 billion pieces of content shared on Facebook alone every month.[8] Willingly or not, every day people are the biggest contributors to Big Data. If we mine the data shrewdly, it provides an unprecedented array of insights into customer needs and behaviors, which can directly help us understand what topics and formats of content to create and where we should place that content. The challenges are data that is stored in different systems and in different formats; much of it is unstructured, and most of us don't know how to analyze and use it effectively. There is not a single standard process or tool to tell us how to approach this.

Measuring content as a function of Big Data starts with the specific issue you want to solve. That issue will inform your measurements. Let's assume our sales team has been working on two major accounts for six months. They have been talking to all the right players during that time. These players have been coming to our Web sites and downloading several pieces of interesting content. To help the sales team, can we predict what content these players will consume next? If we have the insights, we can select and recommend a list of content either by sending it to them via e-mail or syndicating the content in a place where we expect them to find it. To do that, we will need to pull data from different places: each sales engagement in CRM, customer comments, and engagements in various social media platforms and communities, their connections in LinkedIn, their history of content consumption in our systems, the conferences they attended,

> *Measuring content as a function of Big Data starts with the specific issue you want to solve. That issue will inform your measurements.*

and more. Humans can't comprehend or analyze so much data without the use of data management tools such as those from IBM, Microsoft, Oracle, SAP, or Hadoop. With Big Data management and analytic tools, we can even run analysis on how content assists business goals and objectives. This type of analysis is doable but requires resources, budget, and time. Measuring content as a function of Big Data analysis starts with identifying the issues you would like to resolve.

How to scale globally: The cost of running Big Data analysis is still expensive. This is a task that is most likely to be conducted at the headquarters level and the results shared with the local teams.

Services: Enable Internal Groups to Use Content More Effectively

The "service" metric tends to be overlooked by most companies because it typically focuses on content as external customers and inbound marketing. However, well-done content can also be used for internal communications, customer service, management keynotes, and external presentations. Other divisions will sometimes tap your content expertise. Those soft metrics need to be tracked, but there usually is no automated process for doing so. You may have to talk to different teams to gather information manually.

Measure Content as Internal Communications

Some customer case studies and testimonials can easily be used for internal communications. Again, share your content with internal communications managers. I often find some content is suitable for internal communications to rally employees and give them a good sense of how the company is perceived by customers and the market in general. It's yet another way to measure the value of content.

Measure Content as Customer Service

In general, companies' call centers or customer service teams love content, especially if one of the call center's main jobs is troubleshooting. In addition, some call centers' main function is to take orders, which can easily be another channel for up-sell and cross-sell when you have your customers on the phone. A call center's content needs are easily quantifiable. Have a conversation with customer service and call center managers. Understand their challenges. Education-centric and sales enablement content can be helpful for call center and customer service organizations. Review your content list with call center and customer service managers. Let them know what content is available. You may be surprised to discover that some of your content is a great help to them.

Here Is the Reality: Process and Tools Are Fragmented

Measuring the contribution of content to business results or its impact on an organization is hard. It takes deliberate effort and requires processes and tools to do it properly. In addition, it also requires the integration of various systems and data sets in order to get a holistic view. The truth is that relevant data resides in several different systems. Social media metrics come from social media tools, while training sessions are tracked in a different system. Landing page web analytics are tracked with web-related tools. Some of them may not have a direct tie to business objectives. For example: How does having 1 million followers on Twitter impact our sales goals? Is that information even relevant and should it be reported as a metric to management? It may make sense to report that in some companies, but it does not make sense for others.

Even if the tools are connected, you may still need to pull metrics from multiple places. This is typically true for all businesses. As enterprises grow, they acquire a plethora of legacy and new systems that often don't talk to each other. Some businesses don't have budget to invest the right tools to connect all the systems. While this problem exists for companies focusing on one country, the fragmentation of systems and tools is usually even worse for companies operating in multiple countries. There is no quick-and-easy solution to fix this issue.

As long as the technology continues to evolve and new tools continue to be developed, data fragmentation will continue to exist. Once you have a global content plan, measuring business results is a deliberate effort. There is no panacea or shortcut to report out metrics and constantly optimize and measure. It requires ongoing commitment from the team to establish processes and pull metrics from different sources.

Here Is Another Reality: Metrics Are Conflicted

If you are looking at metrics from multiple sources, you are bound to find the data is telling different stories and providing different insights. Here is a great example: marketing research shows brand awareness is in decline, but the media metrics are exceeding expectations and content views on the Web site are in an upward trend. You need to dig into the sources of the data to understand the differences. The research data may be for the last quarter while the media metrics represent only the last three weeks and content views reflect month-to-month comparisons. You need to apply intelligent interpretation to the data. During the regular headquarters and/or geography synch meetings, conflicting data are a good agenda topic to use for discussing possible causes and implications. We may not get to the bottom of it, but we can pinpoint several causes and potential ways to interpret the puzzles and do further research.

In Summary

Align with the Company's Goals to Measure the Impact of Content

Foremost, content plans and measurements need to align with the company's goals. If one of the company's goals is to generate revenue through new and existing customers, the primary job for content is to generate new leads and encourage existing customers to upgrade or purchase more. The measurement should focus on lead generation and customer retention.

Then make an effort to determine the appropriate metrics to measure the impact of content.

To drive sales, you first need to build awareness and educate your customers about your brands and products. Therefore, it's *obligatory* to spend a certain amount of budget on building brand awareness and education. *The question is how to balance the content between awareness and education versus lead generation and customer retention. It begs the question of how to set the metrics and goals for these two initiatives.*

Explain the impact of Content That Management Can Understand

Management cares about sales volume, costs, and revenue. For them to value the impact of content, it's vital to speak their language. Translate the impact of content into sales volume and not jargon such as likes, retweets, fans, and so on. Instead of reporting the total number of followers on Twitter, it's better to report cost per follower (total investment on Twitter divided by the number of followers). Furthermore, you may be able to compare the performance of content marketing efforts across channels to determine which channels perform better.

Also, tell a story. Tell management what you are doing to optimize the quality of content, some interesting tidbits you have learned, and how that impacts the sales and growth of the company.

Integrate Tools to Provide End-to-End Measurement at the Country Level

Tools and processes need to be deployed at the country level. The reality is that tools, processes, and workflows are often lacking or they exist within separate departments yielding fragmented efforts. Most tools are not connected, so you will need to manually pull together incomplete data sets from various sources and spend time to analyze and evaluate your metrics across countries. There is a lot of trial and error necessary to derive useful analytics, which requires a continued effort to connect the dots in order to facilitate end-to-end measurement. Realistically, this adds resource and budget burdens to both the global and local teams. There is no easy solution for this.

Measuring content consumption is easy, but optimizing and measuring the impact of content in the context of driving business and serving internal customers is hard. In the world of global content marketing, there are headquarter metrics and geography metrics. Some metrics are rolled up from geographies to the headquarters and are tracked at the corporate level. Some tactical metrics need to be tracked by the geographies for continuous optimization and local marketing campaigns, but may not need to be shared with headquarters. It's important to agree on two or three hard and tangible metrics to measure the impact of content for both the headquarters and the geographies. It does not hurt to pick some soft and intangible metric (such as usages of content for internal and executive communications) as a worldwide roll up to share with management.

For Entrepreneurs and Small Businesses Owners

► Don't overlook processes and tools. Make necessary investments.
► Balance education and lead generation content.
► Content goals should focus on driving business growth.

For Enterprise Marketing Managers

► Get agreement between headquarters and geographies on two or three metrics to measure the impact of content.
► Metrics tend to be fragmented. Define the process for metrics roll up; source tools and establish processes for monitoring and tracking.
► Optimization needs to be done at the local level and findings shared with other geographies and headquarters.

For Agencies and Marketing Consultants

▶ Understand the metrics that your client will track or help them define what to track.

▶ Help your clients to source the right tools and establish processes. Provide them with several recommendations and help them understand the pros and cons of various tools.

▶ Help them to optimize and measure tangible and intangible results.

SAP's Local-First Content Approach

Michael Brennan, VP of Marketing at SAP, conducted an audit of their English-only content. After reviewing the findings, Brennan and his team realized that a majority of their content was tailored for late-stage buyers. It was mostly about SAP's products and services and why a prospect should choose SAP. There was a content gap to address the earlier stages of a buyer's journey, such as simply helping customers understand what products are available and the benefits of various technology solutions.

Brennan and his team also reviewed how much of the content they produced was actually used by the intended target. Approximately half of the content was never used: no downloads, no page-views and no digital feedback whatsoever. They knew they had a content problem and had tremendous waste in their system. They also found that the local teams only used about 20 percent of the content that was available to them, even if translations were provided in local languages. The local teams prefer content "in country, for country and by country."

Rather than creating content in English, translating to the top 10 languages and hoping the local countries would pick it up, they reversed the model. Brennan and his team built systems and processes that started with local needs. In some cases they decided to stop creating content at corporate and invested instead in helping local countries with technologies and personas.

The SAP Business Innovation blog site (http://blogs.sap.com/innovation/) is a perfect example. Brennan and his team worked centrally with their brand team to define a template for their blog site. They contracted with an external vendor to design and support the site. The corporate team worked with the local team to define requirements on what functionality and processes they needed such as editorial workflows and social sharing guidelines. In order for this process to work, the local team needs to commit to own, invest and maintain editorial planning and content creation. Collectively, the corporate and local teams created a Spanish-language version, a Portuguese version, a German version and other major languages. The local team took full responsibility for managing the content flow and publishing schedule for their respective sites. The editorial plan was locally driven. The content was sourced in different ways with some local sites publishing only SAP-authored content and other sites using curated content. The conversions or "call-to-action" was also a local market decision with clearly identified lead generation goals.

The corporate and local teams meet each month to review success metrics and to share best practices about which content is working, what social approaches each team is using and which method improves conversion rates. Since these sites launched over two years ago, SAP has reached millions of new visitors it would have never reached before—prospects in the early stages of the buying cycle with more localized content. These visitors are generating millions of page-views and ultimately, net-new leads for the business. In addition to the millions of page-views and net-new leads, Brennan and his team reported an Return on Investment (ROI) within weeks of launching the site. They were generating additional leads at no incremental cost. They also saw direct conversions from their online store, and ultimately saw real business close from those leads generated on the site.

While the headquarters team provides the strategy, the business case, the reporting, the technical infrastructure and shares best practices, the local teams are driving content specific to their audience. The local team is responsible for defining the content strategy, the editorial guidelines and the conversion paths that work for their local market. The "local first" approach with clear roles and responsibilities allows both the corporate and local teams to focus on areas of strength. Essentially, collaborative content development efforts have improved effectiveness and served as a model for other business units and marketing functions.

CASE STUDY

Domo's Marketing Spend Optimization

"Content is the foundation of our marketing. It drives everything we do in marketing at Domo," according to Heather Zynczak, chief marketing officer. Domo offers solutions that pull data together in one intuitive platform so that it's easy to see all the information you care about in one place and use it to make faster, better-informed decisions. These solutions can be tailored to the needs of anyone in your company, from the CEO to individual contributors in different departments. Domo discovers insights for its customers by connecting structured and unstructured data that is scattered within companies and puts it in a meaningful context.

Zynczak's marketing strategy is to build Domo as a recognized data expert and focus on solving customers' pain points and challenges. The best way to showcase Domo's expertise and capability is through high quality content. As a savvy CMO, she works through her planning cycle by first looking at the business objectives that Domo is working to achieve and then tailoring her marketing objectives, strategy and metrics to support those goals. Her marketing strategy setting approach is very similar to the process I shared in Chapter 4.

Working with the content marketing team she has built, Zynczak's has clearly identified six global personas of relevance: sales, marketing, CEOs & C-suites, HR, finance, and business intelligence professionals. After the strategy setting and persona alignment, her team determines what they would like to communicate with each persona. Based on that, the content marketing team creates a content roadmap for each persona for the whole year. Yes, the whole year! She calls that, "messaging first, content roadmap second." The whole marketing engine, from outbound to inbound marketing, centers on content-oriented campaigns. She creates the master marketing plan first, identifies key target audiences, lays out messaging and creates an annual content roadmap. As you can see, her content planning process is very similar to the process described in the Chapter 5.

As a CMO, she is held accountable for **hard** metrics such as number of qualified leads and projected sales volume. Her team is on top of the usual measurement suspects such as qualified marketing leads, cost per lead, and design-win pipeline from nurtured leads. Marketing automation tools and a CRM system tracking the effectiveness of marketing is a given. Heather joked that she gets a lot of "data analytics" help, because Domo is a data analytics company. Lucky her! She uses content as an enabler to bring her marketing plan to life and drive marketing results.

In addition to tracking business results, the team spends a lot of time optimizing their inbound and outbound marketing efforts. One example Zynczak's shared with me is that Domo uses multiple marketing tactics to promote their webinars. They noticed that online advertising tended to bring more registrants to the webinars than e-mail campaigns. With that data, they allocated more marketing dollars to online advertising. When the data analyst dug a little deeper by comparing the percentages and numbers of registrants actually attending the webinars from on-line advertising and e-mail campaigns, the discovery was totally opposite expectations. The percentage of people actually attending the webinars from e-mail campaigns was substantially higher than those from online advertising. In other words, e-mail campaigns brought a higher quality of registrants, even though the numbers of registrants were less than that of online advertising. With that insight, they optimized their budget. Optimization is a continuous effort. It does not stop.

Another example of optimization of expenditures is how they promoted one of their hero content items that targeted CEOs: *The 2013 Social CEO Report*[9] published on CEO.com. To promote this "Big Rock" or "Hero" content, they created an integrated paid and social promotion plan, including PR elements. Domo also created several blog posts, charticles (an article with charts) and an infographic to promote this report through social media and paid channels. In addition to launching the report through a carefully timed media relations campaign (aka their content promotional plan), Domo ran an e-mail campaign targeting CEOs and marketers and cross-promoted the report on Domo.com and its affiliated site, CEO.com. Domo built anticipation for the report—which was now in its second year—through a social media teaser campaign. This report received more than 1,000 downloads in the first month as well as more than 500 sales leads and over 65 media placements worldwide, including stories in Bloomberg Businessweek, Forbes, Inc., Mashable, Quartz, NPR, and The Wall Street Journal, to name a few. In comparing the results, Domo saw a 42 percent increase in report downloads from the previous year's study, which it attributes to the increase in the number of top-tier media outlets that carried the news. This report is also used by the sales team as collateral to educate potential customers. In addition, it continues to get cited globally in articles about social media, giving Domo a long tail effect for brand awareness.

Again, Heather would like to know which channels drive the most traffic and leads. The team compared PR data with social media stats and overlaid that with web analytics They discovered that social media promotion performed adequately, but it was the broad PR pick-ups that drove most of the traffic to content downloads. This is another insight that they can use to optimize next year's Social CEO Report promotion. Because this report is targeted to CEOs and C-suites, it makes sense that business media outlet coverage will be more likely to reach them than social media channels.

Moving forward, Heather believes that the future of marketing is data-driven marketing. Data-driven marketing needs to be implemented with right tools and right talents. In that most of the marketing team members are experts in their areas, the role of data analyst or data scientist is essential. In Domo, Heather ensures the data analyst is placed within her marketing organization so that the marketing team is measuring the right metrics and is pulling the right data from across the team and organization to deliver the insights that are needed.

With Domo expanding to other countries, she emphasizes that data analysis needs to be owned by the local team with the corporate's guidance and help. Regardless of countries, CMOs and marketing professionals will need to continuously ask themselves: "What content resonates with customers?" "What platforms perform better with what content?" "What content drives the most leads?" "Does the content make sense for the brands?" Depending on the industries, products and customer preferences, your questions may be different but quantified insights are critical to helping marketing professionals understand the true impact of their marketing efforts.

CHAPTER EIGHT

Skills Needed for Global Content Marketers

"Tis skill, not strength, that governs a ship."

—THOMAS FULLER[1]

It's a Brave New World

When I see a two-year old baby touching a TV and wondering why it does not function like a touch screen, I know the world is changing. When I see a sea of tablets and mobile devices used by passengers on a plane or at a concert, I know the world is changing. When I see my son learn to play new jazz piano pieces and my husband learn to string a tennis racket from YouTube, I know the world is changing. When our family of four sits in the living room watching *Dr. Who*, and we all have our tablets and mobile devices in hand or next to us while we watch, I know the world is changing. All these changes signal a fundamental shift in behaviors.

Behaviors drive marketing. The two-year old's behavior makes me realize future

> *Behaviors drive marketing.*

generations expect all screens to be touch controlled. Content presented on touch screens is different than content displayed on old TV or PC monitors. Touch capability impacts how content is produced. It forces marketers to think in terms of creating content optimized for customer interaction—literally reaching out and touching our content. When I witness the sea of tablets and mobile devices on a plane, I realize we need to create content with a "Mobile First" perspective. Long-form content usually does not work well on the mobile platform, so how do we drive the "Mobile First" discussion with internal corporate and local teams? What is the best way to convert long-form content into a mobile-friendly format? When I watch how my husband and my son learn now, I see implications to the way we publish and distribute user manuals and communicate product comparison information.

> *Marketers must use the right tools, processes and skill sets to keep up with the rapidly changing marketing landscape.*

User manuals are no longer just PDFs; a video format works, too. When I see my kids turn their attention to mobile devices during commercials on television, I wonder if creating commercials makes sense. Interestingly enough, my boys tell me that they still watch commercials and believe commercials still have value; they just pick and choose which ones they want to watch. The way consumers find information, jump from one activity to the next and back, consume content, and interact with technologies and devices is evolving and changing. *We, as marketers, are forced to ask ourselves if we are using the right tools and processes and if we have the right skill sets to keep up with the rapidly changing marketing landscape.*

Something Old, Something New

Consumer behavior and content consumption is ever changing and the rate of change is increasing as new technologies are adopted. Yet, fundamentally, many aspects of consumer behavior and content consumption remain the same over time.

Our hearts swell when we read a good story or see an inspiring image. Our hearts fill with pathos when we witness something devastating. For most of history, word-of-mouth marketing has literally meant marketing content being shared verbally. Now, word-of-mouth marketing is marketing through our accounts on Twitter, Facebook, and other social media platforms. What makes humans tick does not change, but the forms and channels we use to reach people and access those enduring traits have.

It's important to recognize those universal qualities that will always remain the same and those that will need to be addressed differently. Because of this, certain skills for content marketers will remain the same while other skills need to be acquired or learned. After all, the world of content marketing is getting more sophisticated due to the new technologies, new tools, and new behaviors.

Soft and General Skills versus Hard and Specific Skills

Richard Ingram, the content strategist at Ingserv, studied content strategists by surveying 265 practitioners[2] worldwide who documented their skills, knowledge, and abilities from a predetermined set of choices. Ingram created this wonderful chart to highlight the skill sets of a content strategist. It's not a surprise that most content strategists' skills lie in content analysis, development, and management as well as writing and/or editing, editorial strategy, and information architecture. Skill sets focus more on "Produce" than on "Promote" and "Perfect." Because this survey focuses on content strategists, the roles of "Promote" and "Perfect" are likely done by other people or teams within the company. Ingram did a great job capturing most of the skills that a content strategist should possess. Most of the skills in this study were of the "hard and specific" variety: very specific skill sets that are required by content strategists to do their job well. Depending on how you define the role and responsibilities of the content team within your organization, the set of hard and specific skills required will vary (see Figure 8.01).

265 surveyed content strategists were asked to indicate their abilities, knowledge, and skills by choosing from a pre-determined list.

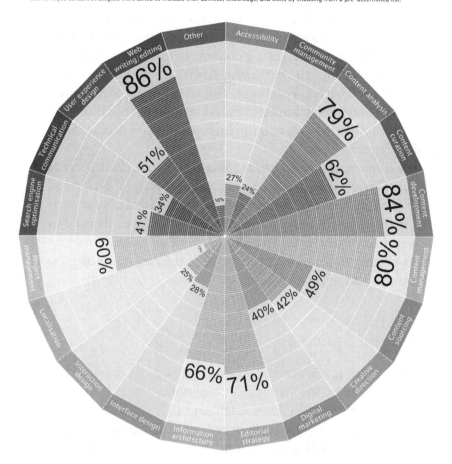

FIGURE 8.01 Where do the world's content strategists' skills lie?

There are also "soft and general" skills that content marketing managers need to complement those listed in the graphic. What are those soft and general skills for content marketing managers? We can approach that question by focusing on another question first: What content challenges are we trying to solve? This is where "soft" skills come into the mix. It's an inherent ability to maneuver the political landscape, influence others to move in the desired direction, and to communicate with senior management in a way they understand.

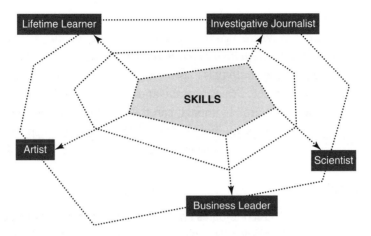

FIGURE 8.02 Soft skills for future content marketers

No matter what content challenges you would like to solve, there are certain aspects of soft and general professional skills that should be developed or possessed by those in content marketing roles (see Figure 8.02).

Business Leader

▶ Corporate communicator: ***Explain content in a way senior managers can understand.*** Tie content benefits to business objectives and quantify the benefits of content in relationship to the company's business objectives. Management does not really care about copywriting, CMS tools, information architecture, or even the editorial calendar. They want to know the results of content strategy and execution. What are the accomplished outcomes or failures of the content strategy you implemented? Elaborate in a way they will understand. Be able to understand what makes management tick and convert content jargon into management lingo that makes sense to senior managers.

▶ Cat herder: Content strategists usually don't have a team. ***Herding cats is a difficult task that usually involves a lot of give and take.*** In addition to tying the benefits of your project to the overall objectives of your "cats," it is helpful to find senior sponsors in the various departments that you'll need to be successful: engineers, marketing communications managers, webmasters, writers, branding specialists, and others.

▶ Budget planner and cost analyst: Content marketing is not free. *It's great to create a content marketing strategy, but you also need to determine how much it will cost to implement the strategy.* If the strategy is implemented, can you tell management the projected sales revenue and growth impact? If there is no sales and growth impact, can the strategy save the company money by being more efficient? The purpose of content marketing is to deliver business results, not a marketing splash.

Scientist

▶ Keep up with technologies and tools: This is challenging to do given that technologies evolve and change so quickly. This is very similar to continuous education credits that you need to obtain every year to keep certification for certain professions. *Setup time to read content marketing blogs and attend industry events to see what tools are developed and offered.* Keep yourself in the loop. You don't need to be technical, but you do need to understand what technologies enable you to do for content marketing.

> *You don't need to be technical, but you do need to understand what technologies enable you to do for content marketing.*

▶ Experiment with new technologies and tools: *Just as consumer behavior is changing rapidly, tools and platforms are changing right along with them.* As our behaviors change, new content management tools are being developed and existing ones are being superseded or upgraded. To keep up with these changes, you or someone on your team should be watching and experimenting with emerging content practices and technologies.

▶ Develop insights from available data: Scientists analyze the data they collect to produce useful insights. I went to listen to Eric Swayne's session, "Scientist to Storyteller: How to Narrate Data," at the 2014 South by Southwest Conference. Swayne did a great job of defining insight, which resonated with me: "*What is insight? It's something that you don't know, you should know and you can change.*" Learn to read and analyze data. Learn to correlate different data sets either by working with your data analyst or possibly by just sitting back and looking at the data differently. What can you tell by examining how many people who subscribe to our newsletter also like our Facebook page? Do your e-mail subscribers also actively comment on your Facebook content? After commenting on Facebook, will that increase or decrease the opening rate of an e-mail they receive? Can we predict what they will comment so we can tailor content to them? Here is a reminder: learn to love data but don't be a slave to it. ***When there is no supporting data, you still have to trust your marketing chops and gut, your artist side***. Everything is about balance and moderation.

Artist

▶ Be open-minded: By working in a global role for over 15 years in which I produced content and worked on creative development, my conclusion is that it's easy to just plain get it wrong. There have been things I was sure would work that just did not pan out. Other creative that I paid little attention to ended up being big hits. In order to minimize misfires, ***you need to understand your blind spots and seek a way to mitigate them***. You won't always be successful, but take advantage of your own company's local teams, if you have them, in order to help see potential problems and opportunities through other's lenses.

> *It's easy to just plain get it wrong. There have been things I was sure would work that just did not pan out.*

▶ Imagine: This sounds like a cliché. However, sometimes it seems like the longer I stay in the business world, the less imagination I have. This is true when I need to be data-driven and communicate with management in a business sense. John Steinbeck wrote, "Did you ever know a man of numbers who did not become small and mean and frightened—all greatness eaten away. ..."[3] You need to find a way to revive your imagination. For my husband, it's reading sci-fi books. For my good friend Elaine, it's about playing cello For me, it's about doing yoga and talking to children. ***We need to actively seek out our muses***.

> *"I'm a student of the game. … You have to learn from the greats that came before you, that's how it should be done."*
>
> **—KOBE BRYANT**

▶ Steal with pride: Stealing does not mean copy, plagiarize, or imitate blindly. ***It's about taking other's ideas, internalizing them, transforming them by applying your own voice, style, and point of view, and making it something new again!*** Of course, don't forget to give the idea owner credit. Kobe Bryant said it well: "I'm a student of the game. … You have to learn from the greats that came before you, that's how it should be done."

Lifetime Learner

▶ Be curious: Doing the same job day in and day out can leave us set in our ways, forgetting to look for new and better ways to achieve familiar objectives. If our job is to generate 1,000 leads a month, we may just continue to use regular e-mail campaigns and blogging, neglecting to search for other, possibly better, ways of doing that. ***"Be curious" can be as narrow as finding ways to do your job better or learning more about our field.*** It can be as broad as pursuing a personal creative journey and blazing a new trail in your life.

▶ Hustle: The marketing field does not stand still. Neither do our customers. They continually learn to use new tools, new devices, and try different ways to consume content. We need to hustle as well. There is not much to it. ***Jump in and get your hands dirty.*** We need to keep learning and moving so we aren't left behind as the world changes around us.

▶ Be resourceful: ***The world is flatter and friendlier.*** While writing this book, I reached out to many industry peers I have never met. Not everyone responded to my questions or requests. I completely understand that everyone is busy and may not be willing to connect with someone outside his or her network. More people than I expected replied and shared their insights and wisdom. Whenever I am given a project I don't know how to do, I search online and try to tap advice from people I know and even some I don't know. That's how we all learn.

Journalist

▶ Reporter mindset: Sometimes it seems as if there is nothing new under the sun. Similar stories or content insights have been shared or told before, yet reporters know how to find a way to tell similar stories as if they were new. The David versus Goliath type of story can be told in the form of a high school state championship, in the Final Four of NCAA March Madness, or in NBA games. It's the same story structure, yet the stories are told through different events. This also applies to content marketing. Consider this example: content about how Gen X uses Pinterest versus how Baby Boomers use Pinterest. Gen X is different than Gen Y and Baby Boomers, so you need to find a way to relate your "news" to your audience and make them see what's new or different. *There is always something "new" to say*, we just need to find a fresh point of view for an old story or find a story that has not been told yet.

> *There is always something "new" to say, we just need to find a fresh point of view for an old story or find a story that has not been told yet.*

▶ Connect unrelated dots: **Connect the dots between your imagination and technology while delivering business results.** I love this 2012 innovative campaign, Hijack, launched by Meat Pack, the trendy shoe store in Guatemala. Instead of e-mailing coupons or sending QR codes, they creatively enhanced their mobile app to "hijack" customers away from competitors' stores by offering discounts in real time. This innovative idea uses pervasive technology to reach their customers. At the same time, it delivers revenue and creates stories for their fans to talk about. Hijack snatched the Bronze and Silver awards in the Mobile category of the 2012 Cannes Lions Festival. Check out this 1:36 video: bit.ly/hijackmeatpack

▶ Tell a story: When adapting a novel for the screen it is necessary to change the flow of a novel to accommodate the specific media. **The same is true when it comes to delivering a message or telling a story in today's fragmented communications channels.** Today's content marketers need to massage the content in a way that resonates with their target audience in various contexts. In the end, it comes down to the ability to bring your stories to life using various formats such as text, video, photos, infographics, and PowerPoint Presentations.

You Can't Know It All, But Don't Be Ignorant

Surround yourself with people who have skills that you don't. You can't be an expert at everything, but it's not an excuse to be ignorant.

By now, you are probably overwhelmed by the skills I mentioned above. Relax. No one can master all the skills previously mentioned. There are certain "soft" skills that you probably already possess and do quite well. Be aware that a mix of skills is needed to be a proficient content marketer moving forward. Surround yourself with people who have skills that you don't. You can't be an expert at everything, but it's not an excuse to be ignorant.

Be Yourself, But Get Out of Your Comfort Zone

Not everyone wants to be friends with data. Some folks can't write but have a knack for creative and imaginative content design. At the end of the day, you need to know your forte. Some of your skills can be fine-tuned and some can be intentionally acquired. Maybe a skill is just not your cup of tea. That's OK!! Know your skills well and know what you can offer. It's also important to get out of your comfort zone to learn something new. You need to find that balance.

Here Is My Personal Journey

I have been blessed by being able to stay at the same company for close to two decades. However, in the year 2014, being "stuck" with one company for so long may be considered a stigma.

The reality is I have jumped around within the same company. I have done different jobs from finance, planning, operations, manufacturing, purchasing, and event marketing to marketing strategy. As I look back now, I am very grateful I have had opportunities to do so many different positions at Intel. It gives me an unique perspective on how a company is run.

As a marketing strategist, I set up strategies and offer guidance for different marketing functions and geographies. To understand our audience and overall competitive landscape, I talk to our sales team, customers, read third-party research, and conduct focus group testing. I make sure that I do my homework and the strategy is backed with data and extensive research from Intel's marketing research department.

This is a good start, but I have come to realize this is not enough! In the past, I would read about SEM, but was not able to make the connection as to how that impacted web traffic, content creation, and the user experience design of a web page. I have a Twitter account but I did not know how Twitter could be incorporated into the overall integrated marketing mix. I also did not know that different writing styles were needed for Twitter communications.

I asked myself: If I could not understand how everything was connected, how could I provide proper guidance to my fellow marketing colleagues?

In 2011, I decided to become a blogger, launched my own Web site, and syndicated my blogs to different social media outlets. I wanted to understand *how things work*. Through the launch and relaunch of my Web site, I learned about user experience, keyword search, web design, and web traffic tracking. Through e-mail campaigns, I learned firsthand that lead generation was incredibly challenging. Through blogging, I learned that having a point of view and quality content matters. Through syndicating blog content, I learned about various social media outlets. I needed to find the ones that worked for me. I even spent my own money buying Facebook ads to get a sense of how to optimize ad buying on that platform.

I have learned so much in the past two and a half years. I still talk to my sales team and my target audience. I still read secondary reports about trends and pundits' opinions. I still work closely with my researchers to conduct primary research for product and audience studies. These are still great ways to learn.

But I've come to realize that the best way to learn is to get my hands dirty. Be in the trenches and just get things done any way possible.

I always wear the hat of a "business leader," but I am slowly branching out to possess the skills of a lifetime learner and technologist so that I can keep up with the ever changing content marketing field.

By the way, I don't recommend any marketer just launch his or her Web site and start blogging. Let me tell you: It's A LOT of work!! It was painful for quite a while. For example, writing a blog on Sunday night to meet a Monday deadline while everyone else is relaxing and trying to get ready for the start of a new week isn't much fun. Unless you are truly committed, don't do it. Yet, I have to say that I learned an incredible amount about content marketing by blogging and promoting my own blogs. "No pain, no gain" is so true!

> *"...to learn and not to do is really not to learn. To know and not to do is really not to know."*
> —STEPHEN R. COVEY

In Summary

It's not easy to be a content marketer. You can probably argue with me it's not easy to be *any* type of marketer in the twenty-first century. A couple of years ago, when I discussed my career development with my mentor, who is a senior vice president of marketing at Intel, she asked me if I want to be a marketing generalist or a marketing specialist. There are different career paths for these two. One aims toward senior management in a general marketing role, while the other leads to management in a functional role focusing on specific marketing fields such as events, social media, research, and so on. My experience demonstrates it's one or the other.

> *It's not easy to be a content marketer. You can probably argue with me it's not easy to be any type of marketer in the twenty-first century.*

To be an expert, it makes sense to specialize in one discipline of marketing. At the same time, having a general knowledge of various marketing functions is how you connect potentially unrelated dots to make content go the extra mile for you and your company. The fun starts when you are able to see how various dots are intertwined and you can make sense out of them.

BONUS

Social Media Manager/Content Manager/ Editorial Planner Hiring Checklist

Ryan Lewis, Founder of Bonfire Marketing, has grown his content marketing agency from a one-person shop to a 25 person organization in less than three years. He was able to manage the continuous growing pains of expanding his business by hiring the right people for the right clients. In other words, he attributes his success to his people.

According to Lewis, "Content marketing is primarily a ground war requiring high frequency maneuvers and nuanced skills to make compelling content on a constant basis." After interviewing hundreds of applicants, he created a list of key questions as part of his interview process. He focuses heavily on what candidates did back in high school or college, regardless of their age. He strongly believes that the early interests and passion reveal traits of a potentially skillful content manager; therefore, some of the questions below may seem unorthodox.

Background Questions:

▶ While in high school or college, did you ever work on the year-book or the school newspaper?

  ▶ People that have been a part of the yearbook or news-paper in school are accustomed to creating relevancy out of mostly mundane content. They typically also learn the value of deadlines early and carry the skills into the workplace.

▶ What clubs were you an active participant in during high school or college?

  ▶ You are looking for clubs that require regular interaction and solving complex problems. Chess, Band, Photography are all very good clubs that attract great potential content managers.

▶ Have you ever held an unpaid leadership position for a shared interest group?

    ▶ It's important to locate leaders and taskmasters. Leaders in unpaid positions know what it takes to "Herd Cats" and drive hard to meet deadlines.

▶ In your previous or current roles, do you participate in activity planning?

    ▶ A person who has helped planning parties, recognizing birthdays and organizing happy hours is usually a good candidate. Also, anyone who is taking lots of pictures at events (look out for them at events for recruitment) can make the transition to content manager smoothly.

Interest Questions

▶ What are your hobbies?

    ▶ You are looking for hobbies that demonstrate curiosity about the world around them. Photography, reading, and political causes are all very good interests for people we classify as "seekers." Seekers are generally very interested in the details of an issue and can create meaning from the mundane.

▶ What are the top three blogs you read?

    ▶ The blogs should represent content marketing industry tactics, general interest blogs with a compelling spin or something representing exploration. The question should be answered very quickly as the right candidates know what they read regularly. National Geographic, Vice, Juxtapose, and Reddit are mainstays for seekers.

▶ If I were visiting your hometown, what three restaurants would you recommend?

    ▶ Seekers make specific recommendations about exploration and deliver answers with passion. Food is a great common interest among people and great content marketers explore and recommend only the best.

▶ What are your three favorite TV shows?

    ▶ This is a culture and tactical question. Sorry sitcoms, but seekers generally don't watch television with laugh tracks. Look for people that like current events, non-fiction or dramas.

- ▶ What is the favorite place you have visited and why?
  - ▶ Travel is typically a big part of a seekers life. If the answer is short, this is probably not an appropriate candidate.
- ▶ Name something you would like to do before you die.
  - ▶ The right content marketer will probably have a hard time naming one thing. After he or she has thought about it for a few seconds, put the question into context and ask about the top three things on his or her list. If the candidate articulates bucket list items with passion, voice inflection and imagination, the interviewee could be a good fit. Seekers usually pause before answers as if they are imagining themselves accomplishing the event.

Screening Questions

Here are some questions that can be sent to applicants to help determine if it's worth pursuing further.

- ▶ In your opinion, what is the best way to measure results in content marketing?
  - ▶ You're not looking for one answer, but how they answer the question. This is a trick question because measuring results is largely based on what is the purpose in the first place. If they attempt to level-set and ask additional questions about goals, you potentially have someone you can work with.
- ▶ Can you articulate how your going to add value to the team? (Purposefully misspelled—"your" to test if they will catch it and mention it)
  - ▶ Details, details, details. A majority of all content marketing is still written. If they cannot make mistake-free content at a high frequency, you might be hiring two people. One for ideas and another to execute ideas flawlessly.
- ▶ How far in advance should a working content calendar be finalized?
  - ▶ This question will reveal their project management methods. Content calendars should be finalized weeks in advance of publishing.

Ultimately, Lewis's job is matchmaking. He not only wants to find the right talent for his company, but also to align a candidate's passion and personal interests to the jobs. If a person applies his personal interests to his regular position, he will enjoy it more and likely be a highly productive member of the team.

Additional questions need to be added, especially if you are interviewing specific marketing roles such as data scientist, data analyst, marketing strategist and more. The checklist provided is a great starting point.

Mr. Lewis, thank you for sharing your checklist.

CHAPTER NINE

Future of Global Content Marketing

"The future ain't what it used to be."

—YOGI BERRA[1]

We Are Proactively Shaping Our Future Through Technology

People are social animals. We like to stay in touch with our distant friends and relatives. Occasionally, we even like to keep tabs on the well-being of our frenemies. We want to be in the know. Because we can't physically travel at light speed or instantly teleport across the country, we invent tools or devices to stay connected.

Once upon a time, postal mail was a relatively fast and cost-effective method of keeping in touch with each other. These days, letters no longer satisfy many of our needs. Photography eventually entered the picture (it's a pun), enabling us to add

> *Because we can't physically travel at light speed or instantly teleport across the country, we invent tools or devices to stay connected.*

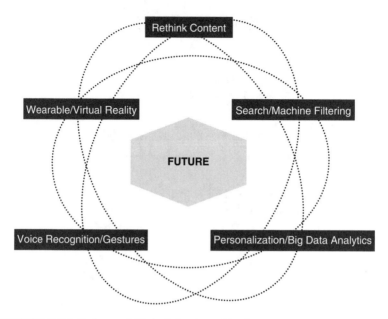

FIGURE 9.01 Future of Global Content Marketing

images to our correspondence. Again, that's no longer good enough. As other tools came along, snail mailing photographs became a less desirable method of sharing information. The telephone was invented, enabling us to converse across distances, in addition to reading letters and looking at pictures. Again, we wanted more. Then, desktop computers allowed us to send e-mail to each other. And the response time was much shorter than using postal mail (see Figure 9.01).

However, neither postal mail, the telephone nor the computer was portable enough so that we could be connected all the time. We continued to invent and create, from personal digital assistants (PDAs) and two-way pagers to those early big and clunky "dumb" phones and eventually Blackberry and other smartphones. To stay in touch, devices need to be connected and easy for us to carry. This did not happen until smartphones and tablets took off in the mid-2000s.[2]

Other factors play important roles in enabling the pervasive use of connected devices as well. The cost of accessing data continues to decrease (OK, not fast enough in some countries) for portable connected devices. Information sharing has become much easier due to the continued growth and availability of the Internet. Search engines help us organize and find information instantly when the need arises. Social media provides platforms for us to voice and share opinions and information. Infrastructure exists to enable a plethora of different devices to communicate with each other. Also millions of apps are available. Apps help us to manage our lives effectively and indulge and immerse ourselves in personal preferences and passion. All these modern marvels have come together at the right time to give our mobile devices compelling power and usefulness. Mobile devices have quickly morphed from simple phones to multifunctional devices. We can use our mobile devices as a form of identification, payment, communication; as a tool for taking pictures, reading, listening to music, setting alarms, monitoring our heartbeats and health, and more. ***Throughout the history of human civilization, we have never created or owned devices that are so intimately personal and allow us to do so much.*** Some of us actually give our devices nicknames because we spend so much time with them. Through our devices, we have become more connected. Imagine that the Earth has a neural network through the advent of the Internet; we have become little nodes of that brain.

> *Through our devices, we have become more connected. Imagine that the Earth has a neural network through the advent of the Internet.*

It must be noted that the "old" technologies haven't disappeared, although some have evolved and morphed. Letters and telephones are still in use, but the ways they're used are different today than they once were. We have the freedom to choose the methods and means to stay connected. Using birthdays as an example: with close family, we may choose a phone call, while for old friends short e-cards might seem most appropriate, and for acquaintances we may opt to send a note via Facebook. The desire to be social will not go away; we continue to change the ways we connect through new innovations. Communication has evolved from postal mail, telephone, computers to smartphones. Who knows what will we invent next and how will we adapt?

Humans and Devices

Technology and devices are changing the marketing landscape and the way we consume content. Every time I see new devices such as the Pebble Watch, Google Glass, the Nike Fuel Band, and other so-called wearables, I can't help but wonder how these devices will affect the way in which we consume content and how these new devices will impact the overall content planning and creation process. I sigh, because it adds another layer of challenges and complexity for marketers like us. I am also energized, because it creates possibilities and opportunities for content marketers.

It's still common to start the content creation process with a PC in mind. Long-form white papers, webinars, and even infographics are designed in formats that are best suited for consumption on a PC. Even now, we place content on our Web site first, then adapt it to fit a mobile phone or tablet format later. That mindset needs to change. Moving forward, it is necessary to determine the appropriate formats that your target audience is most likely to use when being presented with your content in order to design it for easy consumption. Content that works on handheld mobile devices might not work on Google Glass or other wearable form factors.

It will be interesting to see how our relationships with devices evolve. We are adding more and more capabilities to ever-smaller devices. The smaller the devices are, the more portable they are. As devices get more portable, we will use them to help us control and manage our health, lifestyle, personal information, work, and to obtain a competitive edge. In order to avoid falling behind, it's only a matter of time before wearables are the norm for a majority of customer bases and only a small step from there to technology embedded within our

> *It will be interesting to see how our relationships with devices evolve. We are adding more and more capabilities to ever-smaller devices.*

bodies. Relevant content embedded in these wearables can be used to educate us or communicate with us through different usage scenarios. While adding more capabilities to devices, we are also making devices sophisticated enough so that they can begin to anticipate our needs. Devices are learning about us, and we are willingly sharing our personal information with those devices. There will always be surprises, and we can't be certain in which direction technology and our relationships with it will go, but one thing we can be sure about is that we will rely more and more on devices.

Let's take this one step further. 3-D virtual reality headsets are hitting the public consciousness right now and will almost certainly be a mainstay of the near future. The way we interact with that kind of device will dramatically impact how we consume content. If we interact with a virtual world through voice, touch, and hand gestures, we need to produce and present content that allows users to use their voices, hands, and gestures. It's no longer about interacting with a device that you can hold. This new format will have new requirements and require new paradigms. It will no longer be about long-form content or mobile-friendly content; it's imagining content creation at a totally different level. We will likely need to incorporate audio content with gesture and voice recognition using artificial intelligence engines like Siri. Understanding how we consume content through our devices will impact the overall content planning, production, and promotion stages. Our job is not becoming easier, but it certainly will be a lot of fun! *The content marketing opportunities are limitless.* Roles I mentioned in the previous chapters such as artist and lifetime learner become essential as this era of new devices unfolds.

> *Understanding how we consume content through our devices will impact the overall content planning, production, and promotion stages.*

Big, Big, Big Data and Personalization

"There was (sic) 5 exabytes of information created between the dawn of civilization through 2003 . . . but that much information is now created every two days.. . . ." Eric Schmidt,

Google's CEO, shared that tidbit at the Techonomy on August 4, 2010.[3]

The infographic[4] created by Domo provides a quick insight on "How much data is generated every minute?" The infographic is based on 2011 data. By 2013, more than 100 hours of videos are uploaded to YouTube every minute, compared to 48 hours in 2011. Content uploads are not the only way to create a huge amount of data.

Because we are connected, every time we touch any device, there is the possibility that our every step is being recorded by companies who provide the services, apps, or tools. Every search we perform is recorded by search engine companies. Every transaction we conduct through online e-commerce sites is recorded by the vendors' sites. Every quote we highlighted in our e-book is shared with book publishers and authors. That's not the half of it. Even off-line activities, like taking the subway, are being recorded by security cameras and become data. The newer models of cars can track engine performance and report back to the manufacturer. Integrated Global Positioning System (GPS) enables constant tracking of almost every vehicle's and many mobile device's movements, all potentially stored and available to someone.

Clearly, there are privacy concerns involved, but to think the data is not out there is to delude oneself. And, while many people are concerned about their private data being shared, many others opt in, gladly sharing data in return for extra capabilities and features that the data itself enables. Can you imagine all these data integrated into a composite picture that companies or individuals can use to "predict" what we want to do next and what we want to "consume" next? This is already happening to some extent with sites like Amazon.com that predict items you may be interested in based on past purchasing and even browsing history; just as Yahoo.com delivers news it thinks you want based on the data you are voluntarily yielding by using their site. This approach may not always get it right, but it often gets pretty close. The proliferation of connected devices and our dependence on technologies and tools has already created a massive amount of Big Data (see Figure 9.02). It's already happening,

FIGURE 9.02 How Much Data Is Generated Every Minute?

yet most of us don't monetize the data we create, upload, or collect. *Smart and innovative people of the present and future will use the abundance of raw data available from customers and potential customers by leveraging tools and technologies to mine that Big Data to find patterns.* Connecting the dots will lead to new businesses opportunities and profits.

The ability to use this data for targeted personal content marketing will have an impact on the personas we use when creating our global content marketing plans. Personas used to guide past marketing efforts may no longer be valid or may be too general going forward and need to be replaced with new and more segmented personas. In the past, we have looked for the commonalities in subsets of our target audience but Big Data enables us to go much further and understand what makes individuals unique, allowing us to tailor the content to individual needs. As customized and individualized content becomes a necessity, we need to go about creating content differently. In the future, we may need to create data with mathematical modeling in mind. How does my content fit within algorithms trying to index and syndicate through digital media?

> Big Data enables us to go much further and understand what makes individuals unique, allowing us to tailor the content to individual needs.

This information abundance is a very new phenomenon for us. The implications stretch from privacy, policy-making, ethics, psychology, ownership of data, and security to human behavior. Can the company sell our information without our consent? We've all been asked to agree to or to decline the terms of agreement before using a particular application or creating a social media account, but how many of us actually read them? Can friends share the photos that we uploaded to Facebook with others without our consent? Who owns the data that we upload to the Net? What is the role of government, because physical boundaries of countries don't exist online the way they do in the physical world? It will take us a long while to fully come to terms with the implication of all these changes.

Just to sidetrack a little: Ellen DeGeneres, the host of the 86th Academy Awards, organized a group "selfie" photo with A-list movie stars sitting in the audience. She walked out with her Samsung Smartphone (a paid product placement!), arranged the group but handed her phone to Bradley Cooper who took the shot. Who owns the photo? Because it was instigated by Ellen and created using Ellen's phone, ownership should belong to Ellen, right? To my surprise, the ownership of the photo belongs to Bradley Cooper.[5] <<http://www.vanityfair.com/vf-hollywood/bradley-cooper-oscar-selfie.>> The ownership of this type of material is based on laws that have not yet caught up with current technologies and realities. Have we thought about how this will impact the copyright of content that we choose to use for our materials?

Rethink Content In Terms of Raw Components, Not Finished Content

When we think of content, we think of content as completed units in finished file formats such as pdf, wmv, doc, ppt, png, and the like. Because every "piece" of content is a finished unit, it's hard to pull a paragraph from a pdf, an image from a ppt, and a snippet of video from a wmv file to create new content for, say, Google Glass or other form factors.

With Big Data, personalized and customized content is a key differentiator. We need to manage and create content differently. Imagine a system or set of applications that are format agnostic and treat different source content as units of raw material in a big database. Picture content creators in a virtual environment manipulate floating snippets of data as they float around them. Or in the near future, like Tom Cruise in *Minority Report*, we may use "computer gloves" to easily move raw content around on a giant computer screen to assemble and create new finished content optimized for various devices and form factors.

> *Picture content creators in a virtual environment; manipulate floating snippets of data as it floats around them.*

> Moving forward, content creators need to produce modular content components that facilitate others in the task of creating new and repurposed content.

We need to change our mindset of content management. *Instead of creating and visualizing "finished" content, we need to think about how we can cultivate and store content components in a database that can be used and quickly repackaged, reused, and recycled subsets of content for various different devices.* Moving forward, content creators need to produce modular content components that facilitate others in the task of creating new and repurposed content.

Machines Filter Content for Your Pleasure

Let's take personalization to the extreme. In *The Filter Bubble*, Eli Pariser notes that Larry Page was fond of saying: "The ultimate search engine would understand exactly what you mean and give back exactly what you want."[6] The goal is only what the user is really looking for and nothing else. This implies the convergence of search algorithms and artificial intelligence to create an engine that is smart enough to figure out what we really want, even though most of the time we don't know what we want. If Google's vision of searching becomes reality, imagine how that will impact content marketing?

Search is an integral part of our life. John Battelle, Founder of Wired and Federated Media, said it succinctly, "Increasingly, search is our mechanism for how we understand ourselves, our world, and our place within it." Is this affecting our memories? It's hard to remember a time before Internet searching, even though Google was only established in 1998, and Baidu, the Chinese language search engine, in the year 2000. Search is still in its infancy. As it continues to develop, changes in how algorithms determine appropriate results will impact content strategy planning. Eli Pariser also expressed the concern that expert machine filtering of query results that yield exactly what we want and nothing more will paradoxically make us more narrow-minded, unable to see other points of view. That would defeat the hope of many optimists that believe the Internet should help us become more open-minded and receptive to new and foreign points of view. Only time will tell, but the future will likely end up somewhere in between those extremes.

User Experience Becomes More Critical Than Ever

In the future we will not focus only on simple, static content. *Content optimized for wearables and immersive experiences will include gestures, voice recognition, and new triggers so that interactions between the content-serving platforms and users become more intuitive, convenient, and compelling.* Interactive content will become the norm. Intuitive user interfaces and experiences have always been important, but as it becomes harder and harder to catch and keep a potential customer's attention, those interfaces and experiences become more critical than ever. Users tend to scan, rather than read, on the Web. This is likely an even more pronounced tendency for users of wearables and smaller form factor platforms. It's not that people won't read on their devices—it's that now, more than ever before, you have to "earn" their attention. If the audience can't figure out how to consume our content in various form factors within five seconds, they will move on to something else.

All companies that interact with customers through any device need to think carefully about how to make their system, software, products, and customer service user-friendly. User experience will be viewed as a company's competitive advantage moving forward, yet it's still hard to quantify the Return on Investment (ROI) of user experience. Nevertheless, this is not something that companies will, or should, ignore any longer.

> *User experience will be viewed as a company's competitive advantage moving forward*

Near term, what should we do differently?

With more than 6 billion phone subscribers on this planet, mobile devices, including tablets, are the main way people today access content. Steve Jobs called this phenomenon "the post-PC era" back in 2010.[7] John Doerr, partner at Kleiner

Perkins, a renowned venture capital firm in the Silicon Valley, referred to mobile usage growth as the "third wave." "The first wave was about all about PC. The second wave was all about the Internet."[8] The third wave is a combination of expansive mobile usage integrating with geo-location technology and sharing through social networks. Doerr summed up the convergence of three forces, social, local, and mobile, into a ubiquitous term, "SoLoMo" in 2011.[9]

> *During the past few decades, content has been created and consumed on desktops. Moving forward we need to shift to a "mobile first" mindset.*

During the past few decades, content has been created and consumed on desktops. Moving forward we need to shift to a "mobile first" mindset. This may not be comfortable for those of us who have been creating content for desktops. This is beyond responsive design in which an application adjusts itself to scale across multiple screen sizes. Fundamentally, how we use and interact with mobile devices and tablets is different than our interactions with personal computers.

Content design and requirements for mobile Web sites and mobile apps are also different than those for desktops. The creative, length, formats, and tools we use to create content are not the same. Touch, gestures, voice, and other interaction mechanisms allow mobile devices to be more interactive. It's a paradigm shift on how to reimagine new forms of content creation for mobile devices.

For a big enterprise, rallying headquarters and local teams to change their mindsets is a daunting task itself, yet it's a necessary step to move forward. For a smaller company, it's critical to understand how your audience uses their mobile devices to contact, connect, and use your products. Creating content with mobile in mind is an inevitable transition that we all have to make to remain effective.

Go Back to Basics

With all the possibilities and challenges ahead, marketers can become overwhelmed. New devices, new technologies, Big Data, new analytical tools, even new media are coming at a speed with which most marketers find it difficult to cope. I have not even taken into account the scaling of all that into multiple geographies or languages.

Let's consider our predicament for a moment and go back to basics. Why do we create content? You may say that we create content to grow our business. You are right. However, the true purpose of content is to entertain, challenge, and educate our audience. By providing value, we hope to be rewarded with their business. In order to provide value, it is worthwhile to let yourself be guided by the wise words of Thomas Mann, who said, "People's behavior makes sense if you think about it in terms of their goals, needs and motives."[10]

No matter how technologies advance, how sophisticated search algorithms become, how good at anticipating our wishes artificial intelligence programs become, or how Big Data enables personalization of our content needs, everything comes back to:

- ► Start with a great product or service; one that is desired by your customers.
- ► Start with the mindset where you must educate, entertain, and challenge your customers. Start by thinking about your customers' needs. How can you help them?
- ► Plan and strategize your content.
- ► Produce and create relevant content.
- ► Promote and syndicate the content where your customers will find it. It's OK to focus on two or three media channels, but do them well.
- ► Establish processes and tools to measure and optimize continuously.

No matter how the world changes, some fundamental principles stay the same. In a similar way, there are certain sets of values that will always serve as our compass, guiding our life decisions and the way we live. The 4 P's of the Global Content Marketing Cycle stay the same, even though the tactics, tools and promotion channels may be different.

The 4 P's of the Global Content Marketing Cycle stay the same, even though the tactics, tools and promotion channels may be different.

In 2012, Jeffrey Faber interviewed Thomas Friedman at The World Economic Forum. Friedman mentioned that we are in a hyperconnected world.[11] The following statement really resonated with me:

"When I sat down to write *The World is Flat* [in 2004], Facebook didn't exist, Twitter was still a sound, the cloud was still in the sky, 4G was a parking place, LinkedIn was a prison, applications were what you sent to college, and Skype was a typo."

It's amazing how far we have come since the Industrial Revolution. We are living in a world our ancestors could only dream about. But we're not finished yet!

CHAPTER TEN

Epilogue

"Technology feeds on itself. Technology makes more technology possible."

—ALVIN TOFFLER[1]

We Live In the Best of All Possible Worlds[2]

Unlike Voltaire, I am not being sarcastic. Throughout history, there have been a few golden eras that had profound impacts on human knowledge transfers, scientific breakthroughs, seamless cultural integration, and expanded cross-regional trade. The fourth Dynasty of ancient Egypt (Dynasty IV),[3] The Hellenic (Classical) Period of Greece with the Athenian influence,[4] Pax Romana (Roman Peace) of the Roman Empire,[5] the Islamic Golden Age led by the Abbasids,[6] and the Tang Dynasty of China[7] are a few great examples. *The common thread running through all of these golden ages is an emphasis on science, culture, philosophy, and education through several hundred years of peace and prosperity.*

In recent human history, the Renaissance and the age of Enlightenment sparked interest in humanism, artistic revival, and heralded the modern world. The Industrial Revolution is another once-in-a-many-generation era, which not only revolutionized productivity, but also increased the standard of living and shaped the way people worked, lived, and thought. As Harold Perkins, a British social historian, has observed, "the Industrial Revolution was no mere sequence of changes in industrial techniques and production, but a social revolution with social causes as well as profound social effects."[8]

Lucky us! *We are also in a unique, golden era with technology blossoming and impacting every facet of our lives.* How we relate to and interact with family and friends, how we pay for goods and services, how we play (video) games, how we collaborate and work and manage our daily lives are all going through revolutionary transformations on a global scale. Almost everyone is impacted somehow, and future generations will experience even more changes. These changes impact how we search for, consume, and interact with content. *The behavior changes are stealthy and discreet.* The pace of change on some technologies can be like PC adoption, which took decades to permeate the general populace. Other technological changes can happen more like tablet adoption, where the sensation seemed to go from zero to omnipresent overnight.

> Technologies will continue to play an important role in educating, entertaining and challenging our customers.

With a myriad of technologies hitting us, content will continue to play an important role in educating, entertaining, challenging, helping, and supporting our customers. The only thing we know for sure is that the era has just started.

Embrace the Unknowns

Despite everything we have learned in the past, we will never be completely prepared for the future. Content marketing will continue to evolve as new technology and tools unfold. We have no choice but to continue our journey into unchartered territory. It's like maneuvering an outdated ship in heavy fog, and we can't see what's ahead of us, but the current pushes us along and we have no choice but to hang on and steer the best course we can. We can't know for sure if we are headed in the right direction but there are clues and tools that can assist us as we navigate.

The former U.S. secretary of defense, Donald Rumsfeld, has a famous quote that resonates with me: "There are known knowns. These are things we know that we know. There are known unknowns. That is to say, there are things that we know we don't know. But there are also unknown unknowns. There are things we don't know we don't know."

For known knowns, we can rely on and apply to the 4 P's of the global content marketing cycle. For instance, people will continue to be social animals. We are still emotionally connected to good stories and great content regardless of the formats and sources. *We have a strong desire to learn, share, to be challenged, and to be entertained.*

For known unknowns, we don't know how far technology will take us, but we know that technology continues to play a vital role in our lives. *We don't know what and how other form factors or devices will change the way we consume content, but we know the type of content we produce today will probably need to be modified to work well in the future.* We don't know how to predict or guess the next piece of content our customers will consume, but we know we should cultivate multiple sources of data or create a model to make trial-and-error predictions.

For unknown unknowns, we may never fully know the exact steps that our audience takes to find us, because everyone's buying journey is so different across fragmented devices and platforms. We may never fully comprehend the ramifications of Big Data and the endless patterns of correlations and countless dots that we can connect. *We may never fully understand the serendipitous element of content promotion. Let's call that destiny or fate.*

Embrace the known knowns, known unknowns, and unknown unknowns. Be flexible and adaptable. Connecting the dots to uncover unknowns to knowns is what makes our jobs exciting and fun.

Think and Act Globally *and* Locally

> *For content marketing to scale to different countries effectively, we need to think and act both globally and locally.*

It's not enough to think globally and act locally. For content marketing to scale to different countries effectively, we need to *think and act both globally and locally*. The global and local elements need to be taken into account throughout the 4 P's of the global content marketing cycle.

During the "Plan" stage, corporate sets up objectives and strategies, yet the local teams should weigh in and offer feedback. In other words, local isn't responsible for just "acting" and corporate can't do all the "thinking." The local teams must contribute to the overall global content planning or "thinking." During the "Produce" stage, there is active thinking and acting on what content should be produced, localized, and translated from both the corporate and local teams. During the "Promote" stage, the local teams are vigorously acting to implement region-specific promotional tactics to align with the overall content marketing objectives and goals. During the "Perfect" stage, the corporate and local teams may think and act collectively by determining the right measurement tools and metrics to use. In order to perfect local execution, the regional and country teams share promotional results and content measurements with corporate and other local teams.

There are various levels of thinking and acting engagement between the corporate and local teams during the 4 P's stages of the global content marketing cycle. It's no longer "Think globally and act locally." It's a combination of thinking and acting together for the corporate and local teams. Collaborate, communicate, and compromise through aligning shared visions, assembling relevant players, and acting with crisp roles and responsibilities.

Create Content from Your Heart

No doubt, we are in the infobesity era. Individuals feel they have venues to be publishers. Brands feel they need to be publishers. Publishers feel they are THE publishers. However, not everyone can create great content and be great publishers. It takes budget, time, talent, and discipline to do it well.

Producing content is a fun but painful component of global content marketing. Depending on the formats and requirements of the content, we get a chance to exercise our creative muscles. Creating content that resonates with our audience must come from our hearts. Human-to-human connection with a good story that resonates is the goal. It sounds so simple, yet it's so difficult to get it right.

The challenge lies in creating something that is entertaining, useful, or insightful for your audience, yet the content must also facilitate the business opportunities for your company. You need to balance the two sides and create with a purpose in mind. While some content you create can be directly tied to business objectives, other items will have an indirect relationship and can't be tracked or directly linked to those same business objectives, like Costco's cookbook.

Steve Vai, an American guitarist, has a quote that sums up the most important element of content creation: "If you're feeling emotional when you're creating something, it'll sound that way."[9] Reflect who you (your brand) are and put your heart into what you create and you will set yourself on the path to success. That path might be circuitous and lead you through detours and failures. But use the relevant information at your disposal, your experience, and your tools to navigate the best course you can find through an uncertain future.

Final Parting Words

To get content marketing right is challenging enough, especially global content marketing. This book outlines the process of global content marketing from plan to measurement and optimization. The process itself doesn't really mean

Remember, it's people who make global content marketing work.

much; in order to execute it effectively you must assemble a team with shared vision and objectives. That team needs a clear commitment to act and must collaborate through frequent communication and hard compromise. Remember, it's ***people*** who make global content marketing work. Start with global in-mind, be open-minded, and understand local nuances.

Technology will continue to play a critical role in global content marketing. It will impact how our audience consumes and interacts with content. It will also influence the tools and process for content production, promotion, and measurement. As a result, technology also shapes the skill sets required for future content markers.

When I think of the world we live in today, I can't stop thinking about the epic opening of *"A Tales of Two Cities"* by Charles Dickens: "It was the best of times, it was the worst of times, it was the age of wisdom, it was the age of foolishness, it was the epoch of belief, it was the epoch of incredulity, it was the season of Light, it was the season of Darkness, it was the spring of hope, it was the winter of despair. . . ." With a true sense of optimism, I believe that we live in the best of times for human civilization with technologies that make our lives easy and productive. The best is yet to come.

ACKNOWLEDGEMENTS

Wow, I can't believe that I actually finished writing this book! I am not going to lie: writing is a lonely and somewhat painful journey. I am incredibly lucky to have many peers, friends and family helping, supporting and encouraging me on what turned out to be an enjoyable and memorable experience.

Jeffrey Davis, a creativity consultant, helped launch my creative journey, which led to the creation of this book. Ekaterina Walter, Author of Think Like Zuck and the Power of Visual Storytelling, helped me rename the 2 P's of the Global Content Marketing Cycle. Otherwise, the Global Content Marketing would be 2 P's, 1 C, and 1 M. Ekaterina Walter and Joe Pulizzi, Author of Epic Content Marketing, were also generous in sharing their writing and publishing experiences to help me avoid common mistakes. Nancy Bhagat, ex-VP of Intel Global Marketing Strategy and current division CMO of TE Connectivity, provided insightful feedback on how to strike the balance between the headquarters and local teams. Eric Wittlake, Senior Director of Media at Babcock & Jenkins, tore apart my original draft of Chapters 5 and 6 and made me rewrite these two chapters. Thank you, Eric! Stephen George, my go-to graphic designer, translated my dull and hasty sketches of the 4 P's of Global Content Marketing into something wonderful and presentable. Check out his work on http://www.foursclubcreative.com/.

I also offer my deepest gratitude to the marketers who responded to my inquiries, shared their stories with me and allowed me to use their materials. The long list includes, but is not limited to: Michael Brenner, Joe Nevin, Jason A. Miller, Meagen Eisenberg, Monte Wood, Heather Zynczak,

Julie Kehoe, Debi Steigerwald, AJ Huisman, Doug Kessler, Kristina Halvorson, Richard Ingram, Eric Swayne, and Anol Bhattacharya.

Doug Kessler, Pawan Deshpande, and Ryan Lewis were gracious to read the whole manuscript and provided instrumental feedback. My dear friends, Doralisa Palomares and Elaine Mah, read and edited my drafts so many times that I am surprised they still talk to me. I also want to thank the wonderful McGraw-Hill team led by Donya Dickerson for working to have the book available before the 2014 Content Marketing World conference.

Lastly, my dad, Fu-Chu Hsieh, and my mother-in-law, Sandra Didner, are my true inspirations. Sandra completed her first book, *The Conspiracies of Dreams*, at the age of 73. My dad, a retired professor and author of several published political science books in Chinese, is also over 70 and is still writing today. They never stop learning. My sons, Aaron and Joey, were troopers by managing their schoolwork and time effectively so I could focus on writing. Seriously, there was a period of time they didn't see much of their mother. Lastly, a **BIG** heartfelt shout out to my beloved husband, Michael! This poor guy not only had to bear with a stressed and cranky wife (or lack of a wife) working on weekends and late nights for months, but also edited my book tirelessly. He selflessly made my dream his dream. Mikey, I am so blessed to have **YOU** as my lifetime partner and best friend.

ENDNOTES

Chapter 01

1. Costco Web site, FY 2013 Annual Report, http://phx
   .corporate-ir.net/phoenix.zhtml?c=83830&p=irol-reportsannual,
   p. 2, December 18, 2013
2. Joe Pulizzi, *Epic Content Marketing*, p. 15, 2013
3. Jell-O History, http://www.jellogallery.org/history.html, the
   Jell-O Gallery, New York
4. Content marketing, http://en.wikipedia.org/wiki/Content
   _marketing, Wikipedia
5. *Printing press*, http://en.wikipedia.org/wiki/Printing_press,
   Wikipedia
6. Lindsay Goldwert, NY Daily News, http://www.nydailynews.
   com/life-style/health/cell-phone-bathroom-75-americans
   -admit-calling-texting-toilet-article-1.1015634, February 2, 2012
7. Aaron Smith, Pew Research Internet Project, http://www
   .pewinternet.org/2012/11/30/the-best-and-worst-of-mobile
   -connectivity/, November 30, 2012
8. Shea Bennett, *Social Media Overload—How much information
   do we process each day?* http://www.mediabistro.com/alltwitter
   /social-media-overload_b47316, All Twitter, the unofficial
   twitter resource, July 31, 2013
9. Anol Bhattacharya, B2Bento, http://www.b2bento
   .com/2014/04/content-marketing-localization-lost
   -in-translation/, April 16th, 2014
10. English language, http://en.wikipedia.org/wiki/English
    _language, Wikipedia
11. Language Differences, http://www.fulbright.org.uk
    /pre-departure/us-culture/language-differences

12. Islamic New Year, http://en.wikipedia.org/wiki/Islamic
_New_Year, Wikipedia

13. Chinese calendar, http://en.wikipedia.org/wiki/Chinese
_calendar, Wikipedia

14. Rosh Hashanah, http://en.wikipedia.org/wiki/Rosh_Hashanah,
Wikipedia

15. Legal drinking age, http://en.wikipedia.org/wiki/Legal_drinking
_age, Wikipedia

16. Countries where alcohol is illegal, Fox News, http://www
.foxnews.com/leisure/2014/04/04/countries-where-alcohol-is
-illegal/, April 4, 2014

17. Jones_supa, http://news-beta.slashdot.org/
story/13/05/20/1550222/over-100-hours-of-video-uploaded-to
-youtube-every-minute, Over 100 hours of video uploaded to
YouTube every minute, Slashdot, June, 2013

18. Social Networking Statistics, http://www.statisticbrain.com
/social-networking-statistics/, Statistic Brain

19. Nicholas Carr, Is Google Making Us Stupid, http://www
.theatlantic.com/magazine/archive/2008/07/is-google-making
-us-stupid/306868/, the Atlantic.com, July 1, 2008

20. Lloyds TSB Insurance, "Five-minute-memory costs
Brits 1.6B pounds," http://www.insurance.lloydstsb.com
/personal/general/mediacentre/homehazards_pr.asp,
November 2008

21. Ekaterina Walter and Jessica Gioglio, The Power of Visual
Storytelling, p. 8, 2014

22. Joe Pulizzi, Epic Content Marketing, p. 6, 2013

Chapter 02

1. Comic art from Shreyas Navare, Editorial Cartoonist,
Hindustan Times: http://blogs.hindustantimes.com
/dabs-and-jabs/2011/10/09/4-ps-of-marketing/

2. http://en.wikipedia.org/wiki/Marketing_mix

3. The Four C's of Marketing, http://en.wikipedia.org/wiki
/Marketing_mix

4. Richard Ettenson, Eduardo Conrado, Jonathan Knowles,
"Rethinking the 4 P's," Harvard Business Review,
January–February 2013, p. 26

Chapter 03

1. Henry Ford, http://www.brainyquote.com/quotes/quotes/h /henryford384400.html, Brainyquote
2. Henry Ford, http://www.brainyquote.com/quotes/quotes/h /henryford121997.html, Brainyquote
3. Dan, Content Strategists: What Do They Do? http://contentini .com/content-strategists-what-do-they-do/, Contentini, June 18, 2010
4. domain-b.com, Dell launches its first even brand campaign in India, http://www.domain-b.com/companies/companies_d /Dell/20081023_brand_campaign.html, October 23rd, 2008
5. Elena Malykhina, Dell Powers Up First Global SMB Effort, http://www.adweek.com/news/advertising-branding /dell-powers-first-global-smb-effort-106365, AdWeek, September 3, 2009
6. Servant Leadership, https://en.wikipedia.org/wiki/Servant _leadership, Wikipedia
7. Pawan Deshpande, Curata, http://www.curata.com/blog /content-marketing-tools-ultimate-list/, January 16, 2014
8. Brainy quote, Napolean Hill, http://www.brainyquote.com /quotes/authors/n/napoleon_hill.html
9. Direct interview with Meagen Eisenberg, April 4, 2013

Chapter 04

1. Brainyquote, Margaret Thatcher, http://www.brainyquote.com /quotes/quotes/m/margaretth109592.html
2. http://www.brainyquote.com/quotes/quotes/d/dwightdei164720 .html
3. Me Something, Advice from Documentary Filmmakers, https://www.kickstarter.com/projects/1002969621/tell-me -something (a Kickstarter project) Edited by Jessica Edwards, p. 18
4. Yogi Berra Goodreads, https://www.goodreads.com/author /quotes/79014.Yogi_Berra
5. 7 Marketing Personas, https://www.kentico.com/Product /Resources/Quick-Start-Guides/Kentico-EMS-Marketing -Marketing-Personas-Quick-Sta/Marketing-Personas, Kentico EMS Marketing

6. Stephen R. Covey, The 7 Habits of Highly Effective People, 25th Anniversary Edition, p. 9

7. Inc. 500/5000, http://www.inc.com/profile/opus-events-agency, Inc Magazine, 2013

8. Inc. 500/5000, http://www.inc.com/profile/opus-events-agency, Inc Magazine, 2013

9. Inc. 500/5000, http://www.inc.com/profile/opus-events-agency, Inc Magazine, 2013

Chapter 05

1. Kennedy Van der Laan, http://www.chambersandpartners.com/firm/3866/7

2. Tim Asch, Landing Page Optimization, p. 39

3. Jim Lecinski, Google Think Insights, http://www.thinkwithgoogle.com/research-studies/2012-zmot-handbook.html, June, 2012. Referring to a quote by John Ross of Shopper Science.

4. Itamar Simonson and Emanuel Rose, Absolute Value, p. 36

5. Itamar Simonson and Emanuel Rose, Absolute Value, p. 36

6. Kickstarter, FAQ, https://www.kickstarter.com/help/faq/kickstarter+basics#faq_41846

7. Kickstarter, FAQ, https://www.kickstarter.com/help/faq/kickstarter+basics#faq_41846

8. Eric Gilbert and Tanushree Mitra, The language that gets people to give: phrases that predict success on Kickstarters, http://comp.social.gatech.edu/papers/cscw14.crowdfunding.mitra.pdf, Georgia Institute of Technology, February, 2014

9. Eric Gilbert and Tanushree Mitra, The language that gets people to give: phrases that predict success on Kickstarters, http://comp.social.gatech.edu/papers/cscw14.crowdfunding.mitra.pdf, Georgia Institute of Technology, February 2014

10. Eric Gilbert and Tanushree Mitra, http://comp.social.gatech.edu/papers/cscw14.crowdfunding.mitra.pdf, Georgia Institute of Technology, February 2014

11. http://www.clickz.com/clickz/column/2284061/content-mixology-101-a-practical-guide-to-realtime-publishing

12. http://en.wikiquote.org/wiki/Pablo_Picasso

13. Jason Miller, The Sophisticated Marketer's Guide to LinkedIn Webinar, https://linkedin.app.box.com/s /vsstmx5ucdum4dkhbsum, Box

14. Deep Nishar, LinkedIn Official Blog, http://blog.linkedin.com /2014/04/18/the-next-three-billion/, April 18, 2014

15. Craig Smith, March 2014 by the numbers: 80 Amazing LinkedIn Statistics, http://expandedramblings.com/index .php/by-the-numbers-a-few-important-linkedin-stats/# .U03qGOZdVHI, DMR, February 9, 2014

16. Craig Smith, March 2014 by the numbers: 80 Amazing LinkedIn Statistics, http://expandedramblings.com/index .php/by-the-numbers-a-few-important-linkedin-stats/# .U03qGOZdVHI, DMR, February 9, 2014

17. LinkedIn Content Marketing video, http://business.linkedin .com/marketing-solutions/content-marketing/best-practices .html, LinkedIn

18. Jason Miller, Introducing the Sophisticated Marketer's Guide to LinkedIn, http://marketing.linkedin.com/blog/introducing -the-sophisticated-marketers-guide-to-linkedin/, LinkedIn Marketing Solutions Blog, January 22, 2014

Chapter 06

1. Doug Kessler, Diary of a Content Pimp Blog Series, http://www .velocitypartners.co.uk/our-blog/content-promotion-plan-diary -of-a-pimp-3/ Velocity Blog, July 2, 2013

2. Social Customer Engagement Index White Paper, http:// socialmediatoday.com/social-customer-engagement-index -2014-whitepaper, Social Media Today

3. Global CMO Study, https://www14.software.ibm.com/webapp /iwm/web/signup.do?source=swg-smartercommerce-emm&S _PKG=cs_cmo_study, IBM

4. Big Data 101, http://www.intel.com/content/www/us/en/big -data/big-data-101-animation.html, Intel

5. The Mobile Playbook, http://www.themobileplaybook.com /en-us/, Google

6. ITU World Telecommunication/ICT Indicators database, http://www.itu.int/en/ITU-D/Statistics/Pages/stat/default .aspx, December 2013

7. Tutorialspoint, http://www.tutorialspoint.com/management _concepts/the_rule_of_seven.htm

8. Jim Lecinski, The ZMOT Handbook, http://www .thinkwithgoogle.com/research-studies/2012-zmot-handbook .html, Google Insights, p. 11

9. https://www.docusign.com/company, Docusign.com

Chapter 07

1. Fuel Lines, 28 Stimulating Digital and Social Media Marketing Quotes, http://www.fuelingnewbusiness.com /2011/02/23/28-stimulating-digital-and-social-media -marketing-quotes/

2. Steve Radick, Ragan's PR Daily, http://www.prdaily.com /Main/Articles/15d8b5df-a212-485b-aa20-ecaacab209f9.aspx, June 11th, 2014

3. For information about Big Data, see http://en.wikipedia.org /wiki/Big_data

4. A/B testing is described in more detail at http://en.wikipedia .org/wiki/A/B_testing

5. Joellen Sorenson, http://www.savogroup.com/blog /accountable-sales-enablement/, Savo, Smart Selling Blog, September 3, 2013

6. Ben Davis, Tera Data http://blogs.teradata.com/anz/how -much-data-we-create-daily/, November 23, 2013

7. Storagenewsletter.com, http://www.storagenewsletter.com /rubriques/market-reportsresearch/ibm-cmo-study/ October 21, 2011

8. Ben Davis, Tera Data http://blogs.teradata.com/anz/how -much-data-we-create-daily/, November 23, 2013

9. 2013 Social CEO Report, http://www.ceo.com/social-ceo -report-2013/, CEO.com

Chapter 08

1. Brainy quote, Thomas Fuller, http://www.brainyquote.com /quotes/quotes/t/thomasfull378783.html

2. https://www.flickr.com/photos/7819129@N07/5820402523 /lightbox/

3. "The Acts of King Arthur and His Noble Knights" Penguin Classics Deluxe Edition

Chapter 09

1. Brainy Quotes, http://www.brainyquote.com/quotes/quotes/y /yogiberra102747.html
2. Smartphone, http://en.wikipedia.org/wiki/Smartphone, Wikipedia
3. Marshall Kirkpatrick, Google CEO Schmidt: "People aren't ready for the Technology Revolution, http://readwrite.com /2010/08/04/google_ceo_schmidt_people_arent_ready _for_the_tech#awesm=~owED4oGNMrC9JC, Redwrite, August 4, 2010
4. Domo, How Much Data is Generated Every Minute? http://mashable.com/2012/06/22/data-created-every-minute/, Mashable, June 22, 2012
5. http://www.vanityfair.com/vf-hollywood/bradley-cooper -oscar-selfie
6. Eli Pariser, the Filter Bubble, p. 33
7. Jason Hiner, Tech Republic, Steve Jobs proclaims the post -PC era has arrived, http://www.techrepublic.com/blog /tech-sanity-check/steve-jobs-proclaims-the-post-pc-era-has -arrived/4701/, June 2, 2010
8. Seth Fiegerman, Why 'SoLoMo' isn't going anywhere, http:// mashable.com/2013/04/30/solomo/, Mashable, April 30, 2013
9. Seth Fiegerman, Why 'SoLoMo' isn't going anywhere, http:// mashable.com/2013/04/30/solomo/, Mashable, April 30, 2013
10. Thomas Mann, http://www.brainyquote.com/quotes/quotes/t /thomasmann386455.html, Brainyquote
11. The World Economic Forum. http://www.huffingtonpost.com /2012/09/12/thomas-friedman-connected-to-hyperconnected- _n_1878605.html.

Chapter 10

1. Alvin Toffler, http://www.brainyquote.com/quotes/quotes/a /alvintoffl383930.html, Brainy Quote
2. http://en.wikipedia.org/wiki/Candide, Wikipedia

3. http://en.wikipedia.org/wiki/Fourth_Dynasty_of_Egypt, Wikipedia

4. http://en.wikipedia.org/wiki/Classical_Greece, Wikipedia

5. http://en.wikipedia.org/wiki/Pax_Romana, Wikipedia

6. http://en.wikipedia.org/wiki/Islamic_Golden_Age, Wikipedia

7. http://en.wikipedia.org/wiki/Tang_dynasty, Wikipedia

8. The History Guide, http://www.historyguide.org/intellect /lecture17a.html

9. Steve Vai, http://www.quotepiper.com/quotes/authors/steve -vai-quotes/ , Quote Piper

INDEX

ABOUT THE AUTHOR

 With years of experience in multiple global roles, Pam Didner is an expert at creating successful global marketing plans that meet local marketing needs. As a Global Integrated Marketing Strategist for Intel, she led Intel's Enterprise product launches and worldwide marketing campaigns. She also provided strategic guidance on audience development, messaging architecture, editorial planning, content creation, media buys, and social media outreach on a global scale.

Pam has given keynotes, presentations, and workshops at conferences in the United States and Europe. She also shares her marketing thoughts on www.pamdidner.com and contributes articles to the Huffington Post, the Guardian, Daily Crowd Sourcing, Content Marketing Institute, and other publications.

Visit http://www.globalcontent.marketing for supplemental materials about global content marketing.

Twitter: @PamDidner
Blog: www.pamdidner.com